A.A. ALLEN &
MIRACLE
VALLEY

by Steven Phipps, Ph.D.

Tulsa, OK

20 19 18 17   10 9 8 7 6 5 4 3 2 1

A.A. Allen & Miracle Valley
© 2017 Steven Phipps

ISBN: 978-1-68031-115-0

Steven Phipps, Ph.D.
Kimmswick, MO 63053 U.S.

Published by Harrison House Publishers
Tulsa, OK 74145
www.harrisonhouse.com

Dedication

This book is dedicated to the memory of my friend and mentor, Paul J. Cunningham. Cunningham worked with the A.A. Allen ministry from 1965 until Allen's death in 1970.

Cunningham appeared on the platform with Allen in a number of Allen's television programs, and ministered prophetically in some of those programs. He also served as a director of Allen's missionary endeavors.

Without Cunningham's extensive assistance, encouragement, and advice with this project, this book never would have been possible. During much of my extensive research into those who Billye Brim of Prayer Mountain in the Ozarks would term the "old timers," Paul Cunningham was the only person with whom I could freely converse about my passionate interest in the subject of the history of revival movements.

When I told Dr. Brim that, as a result of my studies of the "old timers," I had begun to experience some of what they had experienced, she told me, "That will happen."

The desire is that this account of one of the most significant of the "old timers" will inspire the reader to seek to experience something of the passionate fire which prevailed long ago in a place called Miracle Valley.

Acknowledgements
and a Note on Sources

Several brief or highly focused writings have appeared in the form of articles or book chapters on the life and the ministry career of evangelist A.A. Allen. The present work, however, would seem to be the first comprehensive treatment of this controversial figure.

Three biographical or autobiographical published works were penned by members of the Allen family. During Allen's lifetime, his wife Lexie Allen authored the early biography of her husband which was titled *God's Man of Faith and Power: The Life Story of A.A. Allen* (Hereford, AZ. A. Allen Publications, 1954). This book appears to remain in high demand, whenever the scant remaining copies surface.

According to Paul J. Cunningham, who was a ministry associate of A.A. Allen, Allen was dissatisfied with Lexie's perspective on his life's history. After the divorce of Allen and his wife Lexie, this dissatisfaction was said by Cunningham to have resulted in Allen's own personal account, penned by the credited ghostwriter Walter Wagner.

That book is titled *Born to Lose, Bound to Win* (Garden City, NY: Doubleday & Co., 1970). Cunningham said that this second title represented Allen's attempt to tell his story from his own vantage point after estrangement from his wife.

The third book was authored by Paul Allen. A.A. Allen's son, who wrote an account about what it was like to grow up in the Allen household. His recollections are contained in part of his book titled *Shadow of Greatness: Growing Up "Allen."* Although roughly half of that book consists of new material written by Paul Allen, the rest reproduces earlier writings by his parents. Of the section which was penned by Paul Allen, much of that material largely emphasizes Allen's family life.

John W. Carver, Jr. edited a book titled *The Life and Ministry of A.A. Allen*, subtitled *As Told by A.A. & Lexie Allen* (Westminister, MD: Faith Outreach International, 2010). Carver's book, however, comprises earlier writings authored by both A.A. Allen and his wife Lexie.

The present work appears to represent the first attempt at a truly comprehensive biographical approach to the life of A.A. Allen, with emphasis on his ministry and the legacy of that ministry. Unlike some earlier writings which have been limited in scope, this study is based on examination of a wide range of Allen-related materials and sources.

To the extent possible, this work proceeds from a revisionist historical perspective. Such a perspective attempts, whenever possible, to provide a fresh analysis based on objective examination of available sources. Sources were consulted which were as close to the source and to the actual events as possible, while attempting to maintain objectivity.

Allen was such a controversial character, however, that there will likely be readers who believe the present work assumes an opinionated perspective, no matter which conclusions are presented. That is because even today, well over four decades since the death of A.A. Allen, emotions run high regarding this man and his life and character. Some rush to condemn him, while others seek to justify him. In both cases, it would seem, the facts have frequently become garbled with the telling of his life story over the years.

This seems especially true regarding allegations that his life was characterized by alcohol abuse. Two events marred his life, and extreme controversy still surrounds them to this day. One of those events was an arrest for drunk driving in Knoxville, Tennessee in 1955. The other centered around reports of his death in 1970 which suggested that it was the result of alcohol abuse.

Anything that can be said regarding either event can be expected to inflame emotion. Official records are ordinarily cut-and-dried data sources, but in the case of both these events, some principal facts remain unclear. This is especially the case with the coroner's report of Allen's death, which was the source for his death certificate and for widespread news reports stating that he had died as an alcoholic.

This new biography attempts to examine those events as objectively as possible. At the same time, however, it is recognized that, at least in the case of the coroner's report, even the official records seem to raise questions more than provide answers.

This study will, however, examine evidence that does not appear to have been previously considered. Readers will still have to form their own interpretations, but at least they should be better equipped to do so because of the new data which is introduced here.

As an author of published historical research on other subjects, I have generally depended largely on newspaper accounts. In the case of Allen, however, such sources have sometimes been of only limited utility. Surprisingly few articles appeared, with the exception of large numbers of notices and ads pertaining to specific ministry appearances and associated with his death.

I am grateful to the late Paul Cunningham, who had been a member of Allen's staff and who appeared with Allen in a number of the latter's television programs, for providing Allen materials from his collection. In addition, Cunningham spent countless hours sharing his recollections of Allen's life and ministry.

I would also like to express appreciation to musician Richard Page for his valuable insight into the life and ministry of A.A. Allen. Page, who played organ in Allen's meetings, appears on the platform in many of Allen's television programs as a member of Allen's worship team.

Other sources which have proved useful include articles about Allen which appeared in various issues of *The Voice of Healing* magazine in addition to those published in Allen's own *Miracle Magazine*.

Books and other publications (including study courses and pamphlets) written by Allen or associates and published by the Allen ministry were of course consulted, in addition to a vast number of video and audio recordings associated with A.A. Allen and his ministry organization. Those recordings are primarily of Allen's television and radio broadcasts or of record albums produced at Miracle Valley, which was Allen's ministry headquarters.

Actual ministry records and documents which reveal much of the nature and character of A.A. Allen and his ministry do not appear to be abundant. Unconfirmed reports suggest that the bulk of the official ministry records were intentionally destroyed. after Allen's death.

This book briefly considers the legacy of Allen's ministry following his death in 1970. Also included is the continuing saga of Miracle Valley, which had been Allen's ministry headquarters in southern Arizona.

The 1982 gun battle at Miracle Valley, for example, was the subject of its own book-length treatment in William R. Daniel, *Shootout at Miracle Valley* (Tucson: Wheatmark, 2009). The "shootout" is also the subject of a documentary titled *Gun Shot Valley* by Thomas Javier Castillo, but at this writing, this appears to be a work in progress.[1]

A number of individuals provided significant assistance in the preparation of this volume. In particular I would like to express gratitude and appreciation for the extensive assistance provided by Paul Cunningham, who formerly worked with Allen's ministry organization. I was preparing for a visit to his home when his wife informed me of his unexpected death on Christmas Day in 2009.

Cunningham provided extensive oral history information regarding Allen's ministry and Miracle Valley. He joined Allen's ministry at Miracle Valley in 1965 and, as already mentioned, appeared on the platform with Allen in a number of the latter's 1960s television broadcasts. Occasionally he ministered prophetically in those programs.

Additional information was furnished by Diane Langevin of Miracle Valley Arizona Ministries, by Martha Martin, who worked with Paul Cunningham's ministry and other related ministries, and by David Hollis, who was instrumental in establishing A.A. Allen's business office in Allen's early days in Dallas.

The Flower Pentecostal Heritage Center (FPHC) at the Assemblies of God denominational headquarters in Springfield,

Missouri houses a large collection of Allen-related published materials which have been of particular help. These materials consist of not only media items produced by Allen's ministry, but files documenting Allen's relationship to the Assemblies of God prior to his separation from the denomination in 1956.

In particular, Director Darrin Rodgers and Archivist Glenn Gohr of the FPHC have provided not only valuable research assistance, but encouragement regarding this and other revival history research projects. I would like to especially thank Darrin Rodgers for providing access to files pertaining to A.A. Allen which are ordinarily closed. I would also like to thank Billye Brim of Prayer Mountain in the Ozarks for her encouragement with my research in general into the history of revival movements.

Additional general research assistance was provided by the staff of the History and Genealogy Department, formerly known as Special Collections, of the St. Louis County Library in Frontenac, Missouri. I am particularly grateful to Ruth Ann Hager, Chris Flesor, and Larry Franke of the library staff for their valuable assistance. Thanks also to Raleigh Muns, Reference Librarian at the University of Missouri - St. Louis.

As can be expected with any extremely intensive research project, I have been profoundly changed as a result of my immersion into the world of "God's man of faith and power," evangelist A.A. Allen. Regardless of the stand one might take with regard to the issues and controversies which surrounded his life, one fact has emerged as an incontrovertible facet of his life and ministry: That ministry had unique qualities, and wielded profound and far-reaching influence. This is precisely why that ministry remains controversial, even today.

In addition, a lasting legacy has come out of the ministry of A.A. Allen. Various 20th century ministries could trace their ministry beginnings to Zion, Illinois, the community founded by equally controversial healing evangelist John Alexander Dowie. Those ministries included the likes of F.F. Bosworth, John G. Lake, and Gordon Lindsay. In similar manner, a number of significant ministry figures were, at one time, associated with A.A. Allen's ministry headquarters at Miracle Valley. These include R.W. Schambach, Jerry Bernard, Nancy Harmon, and a true legend of gospel music, Goldia Haynes.

Regardless of his shortcomings, Allen taught that we should stretch our faith and believe God for the seemingly impossible. The continuing interest in "God's man of faith and power" suggests that hearts are still hungry for accounts of individuals ministering in the power of God.

Table of Contents

Chapter 1:

A Call to Ministry

From the late 1940s, through the '50s and into the '60s, America entered into an era characterized by hugely popular healing ministries and healing revival services. Those meetings were often tent-based.

Seemingly countless individuals suddenly emerged from obscurity during that era, and entered national and even international prominence as what were known as "healing evangelists." A.A. Allen was simply one of many. Allen was, however, one of the most criticized and controversial of all of the more prominent evangelists, arguably more so than any of his peers. Some of the miracles claimed in his meetings, though, were among some of the most extreme.

In fact, he has been called "the most notorious practitioner of the radical Pentecostal healing and deliverance ministry."[2] He was characterized late in life as "the last of the red-hot healers."[3]

His ministry organization has been referred to as "the General Motors of the revival circuit."[4]

Yet, it would seem, for every accusation or critical label hurled against him by his detractors, some evidence would seem to support alternative views. For that reason, even some of the most fundamental aspects of his life are still topics of debate.

Largely through his TV and radio ministry, A.A. Allen became one of the best known of the healing evangelists associated with the post-World War II healing revival movement in America. Although he consistently went by the name A.A. Allen in ministry, Allen's full name was Asa Alonzo Allen.

Few called him "Asa," however. For the masses who attended his meetings or tuned him in via radio or television, he was simply "evangelist A.A. Allen," known as "God's man of faith and power."

Most of those who viewed his television programs from the 1950s until the time of his death in 1970 saw him in black and white, but Allen had red hair. When he died, he was 5 feet, 9 inches tall and weighed 160 pounds.[5] Shortly before Allen's death, a newspaper reporter observed that he was wearing "flashing cufflinks in a hot pink shirt" while "pacing in bellbottom trousers."[6]

Family Background

A.A. Allen was born March 27, 1911 in a tiny village in northeastern Arkansas called Sulphur Rock, located in Independence County. At least a couple sources refer to him as having been "born into poverty."[7] His parents were Asa O. Allen and his wife Leonia (Clark) Allen.

An Independence County, Arkansas marriage license shows them as A.O. Allen and Leonia M. Clark.[8] He was 23 at the time, and his bride was only 15 years old. They were issued the license on February 6, 1892.

The 1910 census shows the couple as living on Mills Street in Sulphur Rock. Forty-three-year-old A.O. Allen was working as a laborer in a sawmill.

That census barely missed son A.A. Allen, who was not born until the following year, 1911. He then appears in the 1920 and 1930 censuses in the household of his mother's new husband, John Bailey.

There he is listed in 1930 as a son but in 1920, more accurately, as a stepson. Bailey's wife, who was Asa's mother, is referred to variously as Leonia, Leonina, and Leona, depending on which record one consults.

Her death certificate calls her Leonia. The 1930 census suggests that John Bailey was 32 years old at the time of his first marriage, but that Leonia, as we already knew, was only 15.

In 1920, the family was living in Marion Township in Jasper County, Missouri. This was in the southwest Missouri Ozarks. Bailey was working as a laborer for a gravel company. By the time of the 1930 census, they had moved into an adjacent county, Lawrence County, where they lived in Lincoln Township.

The family owned a farm worth $1,600. According to the census, they did not own a radio, presumably because they were too poor to afford one. Asa A. Allen, Leonia's 19-year-old son, is listed as living at home, but without a job.

The death certificate for Leonia Bailey shows that she was born as Leonia Clark on April 26, 1876 in Highrock, Arkansas.

Her parents, Frank and Minerva Clark, were both born in Batesville, Arkansas. When she died on October 17, 1939, she had divorced her second husband.

The sources who said that Allen was "born into poverty" were undoubtedly correct. When his mother died, she had been living in the County Home, a facility which was commonly referred to as the local "poor house." This was in Lawrence County, Missouri.

A 2006 oral history interview[9] regarding Mt. Vernon, the county seat of Lawrence County, mentioned the County Home:

> On the south side of town, just down from the IOOF cemetery, is a beautiful house that was the former County Farm, or better known as the Poor House.

Leonia was buried in Eastlawn Cemetery in Springfield, Missouri.

Later in life, A.A. Allen surfaced in Colorado. When Lexie Scriven, his wife to be, first met him, the whispered rumor was that he was from Barrel Springs. This was a locally notorious place in Colorado, hardly large enough to qualify as a town or even as a village. Evidently a prevailing local impression at the time was that Barrel Springs was, at least in part, home to disreputable elements.

Lexie was from a prairie area near Lamar, Colorado known as Clearview District. Residents tended to follow a cultural legacy established by earlier Dunkard Brethren settlers. This resulted in a prevailing lifestyle which Lexie characterized as conscientious, honest, and hard-working.[10]

Allen, on the other hand, lived at the comparatively wild Barrel Springs, an area to the south which deservedly did not enjoy as good of a reputation. Lexie described this neighborhood as having been the location of a number of hideouts for Prohibition-era bootleggers.[11] This was the social context in which Allen seemed to thrive for a time.

Lexie Scriven appeared in the 1920 census in Granada, Colorado, where she was living with her brother Joseph and their parents, Elmer C. and Cordelia Scriven. Granada is a tiny town in Prowers County, located near the old Santa Fe Trail. Even as late as the time of the 2000 census, the town's population was only 640.

Lexie's father Elmer Scriven, or more fully Elmer Craig Scriven, was listed in 1920 as a farmer. His daughter Lexie's age at the time appears to have been 3 years and 9 months.

Ten years later, in 1930, she appeared again in the census. This time she was living in Carlton, also in Prowers County, where her age was listed as 14. Carlton is a populated place, but just barely so. The town is located between Granada and the much bigger town of Lamar.

A Move to Missouri

By 1934, Allen had moved to Missouri, where he was living at his mother's home near a small town called Miller. Here he pursued a lifestyle which did nothing to suggest his eventual career as a minister. Instead, he set up a still and operated a dance hall in his mother's home.

Seemingly completely out of character, however, one night in June he visited what was known as Onward Methodist Church in Miller. He returned the next night, and there he had a born-again experience. One source refers to this church as having been "a 'tongues-speaking' Methodist church."[12]

Miller is a very small town in Lawrence County in southwest Missouri. Onward Methodist Church is located about eight to nine miles east of Miller. Satellite views show a small building with an even smaller gravel parking lot.

That was in June of 1934. In September of that year, Allen moved back to Colorado, because he couldn't find work in Missouri. Before his return, Lexie Scriven heard that "the Allen boy" was returning, and the prevailing rumor was that he had "gotten religion."

Lexie, whose number one drive by this time was her dedication to God, asked herself, "Lots of people have 'got religion.' I wonder if he's got SALVATION?"[13]

After his arrival back in Colorado, where he went to work for a local rancher, he tried to find someone with a similar spiritual focus, experience, and orientation. The only person in the area who seemed to fall into that category was "that Scriven girl," as his rancher employer referred to her.[14]

When the two were able to meet for the second time, after his return to Colorado, she was disappointed to find that he had become involved with a Methodist church. Methodism could be rather staid and formal. Perhaps Allen was Christian in name only.

Still, locals had kidded her about her interest in Allen, pointing out to her that he was now as "religious" as she was. Lexie told herself, though, that she had no interest in someone who merely had "Methodist religion."

Asa assured her, however, that he had experienced much more than just denominational religion. "But I'm really Pentecostal," he assured her. "I was saved in a Methodist church, but I got filled with the Holy Ghost at the Pentecostal meeting."[15]

This evidently met with Lexie's approval. The two began spending much of their time together. Then, however, Allen returned to Missouri to help his mother to sell her property and prepare to move to Idaho.

The Move to Idaho

Apparently it was in 1935 that Asa Allen moved into Payette County, Idaho with his mother. One quirk of the 1940 census is that it not only listed where people were living in 1940, but indicated where those same people had lived on April 1, 1935 as well. On that date, according to the census, he had been living in the same location, Payette County.

The city of Payette was a small town in a tiny county situated adjacent to the Oregon state line. In fact, this is Idaho's smallest county. In writing to Lexie, he noted, "Here we are in Payette, Idaho. We got into town yesterday afternoon, and rented a cabin. Last night, I found a place to go to church."

A few months later, Lexie Scriven responded to what she believed was a call to ministry by entering Bible college. Her choice of schools indicated her commitment to the Assemblies of God denomination. This denominational adherence made sense to A.A. Allen at the time, but later, as Allen's ministry developed into a phenomenon of major proportions, it would prove to be a wedge driven between Asa and Lexie.

In October 1935, Lexie began attending Central Bible Institute by herself. This college, which was later called Central Bible College, was operated by the Assemblies of God. CBC operated as a coed Bible college until its campus closed its doors in 2013. The college was subsequently absorbed into Evangel University, also operated by the Assemblies of God.

All those months of writing back and forth finally culminated in marriage. Asa Allen and Lexie Scriven returned to Colorado, where they wed. The ceremony was performed on September 19, 1936 in Lamar, in Prowers County. Asa was 25 and Lexie was 20.

The couple's orientation was decidedly Assemblies of God, which may have been more Lexie's idea than Asa's. Their wedding ceremony was performed by an Assemblies of God minister from the town of Holly, also in Prowers County. He was Rev. Earl Brotton.[16]

Lewis Earl Brotton was born September 5, 1899, and was ordained by the Assemblies of God on February 15, 1935. He died December 3, 1971,[17] which was the year after Allen died. The 1939 Assemblies of God directory shows Brotton as a pastor in Holly, Colorado.[18]

After the wedding, the couple drove back to Missouri. The two wanted to attend Central Bible Institute, but the money they would have spent doing so was used to nurse Asa's mother back to health. She had supposedly become malnourished in her son's absence.

Both A.A. Allen and his new wife were eager to enter ministry, and the way to do so, they thought, was to enter Bible college. Asa quickly found discouragement and a bit of disillusionment, however, as he tried to follow this approach. The school they chose, Central Bible Institute in Springfield, Missouri, needed ample funds upfront, more money than Asa was able to come up with at the time.

He asked the school to give him a little time as he looked to God. He let them know that he was confident that, through his trust in God, the finances would be provided. The college, however, would not budge.

Allen did finally become licensed with the Assemblies of God in 1936,[19] according to one source. The denomination's records at the Flower Pentecostal Heritage Center, however, date his ordination as February 13, 1942.[20]

Chapter 2:

Building a Ministry

Asa and Lexie Allen's son James was born in 1937. A.A. Allen later told of how, when James was still a baby, he developed a problem with one of his eyes. He appeared to have an infection which left his eye looking red, with a discharge. As the days followed, it appeared that James had become completely blind in one eye, and that the eyeball was shrinking.

Asa and Lexie took James to one revival meeting after another to be prayed for, as they attempted to believe for his healing. Finally, however, at a meeting in eastern Colorado, a group of ministers laid hands on James. At that moment, A.A. Allen knew that God had heard their prayers.[21]

At the time, the baby was asleep, with his eyes closed. The following morning, however, while Asa was building a fire, he heard his wife shout from the nursery, "It's done! It's done!" Both eyes looked exactly the same, and James was healed.[22]

In later years, A.A. Allen recounted two experiences from his younger days as a Christian, experiences which prepared him for ministry as "God's man of faith and power." One of those was the experience he details in his book, *The Price of God's Miracle Working Power.* The other was a nightmarish experience during which he felt constant anxiety and depression, but couldn't figure out why. Nothing he did seemed to shake it.

He detailed that latter experience in a spoken message he titled "My Cross." That story was released in book form in 1957.

Holiness and Pentecostal groups of the late 19th and early 20th centuries commonly believed in a separate sanctification experience subsequent to the born-again experience. Although A.A. Allen may not have referred to such an experience by name, he certainly talked in terms of what some might define as a sanctification experience in his spoken ministry.

That experience is described in his best known book, *The Price of God's Miracle Working Power.* There he details an experience early in his ministry - evidently sometime around 1940[23] - in which he secluded himself and sought God for power in ministry. He sought to minister healing with power and authority.

The answer eventually came: If he wanted to minister healing and deliverance with the power of God in manifestation, Allen would need to rid his life of personal sins. Those sins, in Allen's terms, might be called "besetting sins."

This concept is further developed in another publication by Allen, a booklet called *My Besetting Sin!* The title is based on a passage in the Biblical book of Hebrews (12:1) which refers to the need to "lay aside every weight, and the sin which doth so easily beset us." Allen addressed his readers by declaring to them,

I'm talking to you this morning about your besetting sin. The sin that besets you. The sin that sets you back, that holds you down, that ties you, that puts chains around you, that puts fetters on you, that binds you, that keeps you from running the race that God has laid out ahead of you.[24]

He made a further appeal in the foreword to the booklet. There he noted that accepted levels of holiness, even levels that are customary in the church, might not be enough if one wants to experience everything which God has for his people:

You must rid yourself of that besetting sin!

"Everybody does it," is not sufficient excuse!

"Everybody" is not accomplishing the thing God has called you to do!

If you go along with "everybody," you will never fulfill your calling. And when you stand before Him in the judgment, you will stand alone, to give an account of His personal call to YOU![25]

This concept of ridding oneself of a "besetting sin" is remarkably similar to one of the four "principles" urged by Evan Roberts at the onset of the Welsh Revival of 1904. These were principles Roberts insisted must be put into practice in order to experience what he termed "the grand blessing" of revival.

Those four requirements, as taught by Evan Roberts, were that (1) we must confess to God any sin not previously acknowledged, (2) we must rid ourselves of anything in our lives which is doubtful, (3) one must yield to the promptings of the Holy Spirit, and (4) we must openly and publicly confess Christ.

Allen's experience in which he claimed to have been supernaturally taught of the need to rid himself of every "besetting sin" marked a turning point in his life. It was presumably because of this that he left the pastoral ministry and became a singing and healing evangelist.

The 1940 census shows Asa Allen and family living in New Meadows "Precinct" in Adams County, Idaho. Adams County is on the west central edge of the state, adjoining eastern Oregon. The community of New Meadows is, even today, a tiny town, with its population in 2010 at only 496.

The town is located on the Little Salmon River, at the southern end of the Meadows Valley. New Meadows is situated at the junction of U.S. Highway 95 and State Highway 55. On May 3, 1940, A.A. and Lexie Allen and their children were living on Highway 95 in a home they owned which was worth $400.

Although Lexie had finished four years of high school according to that census, Asa only had an 8th grade education. This census reveals where they had been living about five years earlier: On April 1, 1935, Asa was living in Payette County, Idaho, while Lexie was in Springfield, Missouri. This would have been while she was attending Central Bible Institute.

Allen's occupation is listed in the 1940 census as "Preaching Ministry," which he was conducting on his "own account." The number of weeks he worked during 1939 was reported as 52, which yielded an income of $500 for the entire year.

Children of Asa and Lexie are listed in that census as two-year-old James C. (who would have been born about 1938), born in Colorado; one-year-old Mary E., born in Idaho, and two-month-old John, with a middle initial that is unclear. John's birthplace was given as Idaho, but with this word crossed out.

Allen's Early Ministry

A.A. Allen does not appear in Assemblies of God ministerial directories until 1942. Then he is listed as "Asa A. Allen," with address as P.O. Box 502, Clifton, Colorado.[26] Clifton was nearly on the Kansas state line.

The Assemblies of God weekly magazine *The Pentecostal Evangel* included a brief mention of Allen in its issue of April 25, 1942. There it was noted that Asa A. Allen of Clifton, Colorado, was among those whose names "were added to the General Council ministerial list during the months of February and March" of that year.[27]

The 1943 minister directory of the Assemblies of God lists the address for "Asa A. Allen" as Box 111, Julesburg, Colorado.[28] This was near the northeast corner of Colorado. The only Assembly of God church listed in the same town in that directory is "Asamblea de Dios," pastored by Josue Ortiz,[29] but Allen had already entered a traveling ministry by this time.

The itinerant ministry of A.A. Allen was already being promoted as early as 1945. One of Allen's early significant campaigns was held in Newcastle, Wyoming. Newcastle is the county seat of Weston County, and is located nearly at the South Dakota state line.

In January of that year, a display ad appeared in a Newcastle, Wyoming newspaper, urging readers to "Follow the crowds to the 'Victory Revival'" being conducted by A.A. Allen, described as an "Outstanding Prophetical Preacher."[30]

Even this early, one night during his Sunday-to-Sunday campaign ("Nightly Except Saturday") was devoted to healing. That night's meeting was promoted as a "Divine Healing Night."

This series of meetings began January 7th at the local Assembly of God church where L.E. Wead was pastor.

That ad appeared in the *News Letter Journal* on January 4, 1945. A few days later, on January 18th, another large display ad appeared in the same paper. This one announced that Allen's "Victory Revival" would go into its "Fourth Successful Week," and that this was "by popular demand."

A news article reiterated that this extra week was in response to unprecedented demand.[31] This was said to have especially been the case during Allen's earlier Jubilee service. This was when all the seats that could be found in the basement were moved upstairs to accommodate the growing crowds.

During these meetings, Allen would be "Calling America Back to the Bible and God," according to the ad. Allen would not just preach. Instead, participants could expect to "witness the power of God in manifestation to save from sin, to fill with the Holy Spirit and to Heal sickness."

Allen was scheduled to speak on the subjects "When the Stars and Stripes no longer wave over America," "The world's greatest catastrophe," "When it comes God's turn to laugh," and "The black verse of the Bible." Luke 23:30 notes that, according to the King James translation, "Then shall they begin to say to the mountains, Fall on us, and to the hills, Cover us." Allen alluded to this one night but drove the point home by specifically relating the scripture to his local audience. He announced to the public of Newcastle, Wyoming, that he would be speaking on the subject, "When Newcastle prays for the Black Hills to fall upon them."

"Jubilee Night," scheduled for Tuesday, would feature "the best musical talent in the state." In keeping with a common custom of the era, a "chalk talk" would also be featured. Chalk talks ordinarily involved creating a drawing, usually with colored chalk, while preaching or while relating a Bible story. As a further enticement, a "beautiful pastel chalk drawing" was to be awarded each evening to whoever was responsible for bringing the most people to the meeting.

In September of the same year, 1945, Allen was back in town again. The same paper ran another large display ad announcing an "Open Door" Revival featuring A.A. Allen, to begin on October 1st. His sermons in his earlier visit, beginning in late 1944, were said to have been "heart searching," with the implication being that audiences could expect the same. Capacity crowds were expected for his new series of meetings.

In this crusade as in the previous one in Newcastle, sermon topics were publicly announced in advance. This time, the subjects were decidedly prophecy-focused, while relevant to what was, in those days, contemporary society. These included "The White Horse Rider of Revelation 6:2," "The Red Horse of Revelation Six Four," "When Death Rides the Pale Horse Across the U.S.A.," "World War Number Three in Prophecy," "Souls for Sale," and "God's Controversy with the Nations." Again, "special prayer for the sick" would be included.

A Move Toward "Signs and Wonders"

Allen became pastor of a church in Corpus Christi, Texas, in 1947.[32] He is said[33] to have attended an Oral Roberts meeting in Dallas in late 1948,[34] at first skeptical. As he witnessed first hand the type of healing ministry that was being conducted involving capacity crowds in Roberts' tent, however, Allen quickly became convinced that Roberts' ministry was of God.

Not only that, but at the time, most church buildings open to Allen were undersized. Allen developed the conviction that tent meetings would be a way to freely pursue his own ministry outside the confines of tiny church buildings, with what he saw as sectarian doctrinal quirks and limitations.

With that belief and with the refusal of his Corpus Christi church to support him in radio ministry, as the story goes, Allen decided to enter an itinerant ministry similar to that of Roberts. He appears to have had no real encouragement to do so. Certainly, the members of his congregation did not support the idea.

Soon afterward, Allen held a revival in Long Beach, California, which closed near the time a May 14, 1949 newspaper display ad appeared.[35] Allen's sermon titles had been gradually becoming more provocative. That ad announced that he would be speaking on the subject of "Spiritual Suicide." Allen was being referred to at the time as an "Evangelist, Musician, Singer" from Corpus Christi, Texas.

He was speaking at Revival Center Church, where Robert E. Reid was the pastor. Allen would continue to use churches, largely Assemblies of God, as venues for his meetings, but he didn't abandon the idea of getting out of the churches and ministering in tent crusades. In fact, he was to buy his first tent not long afterward, in 1951.

In the meantime, Allen was holding meetings in churches, meetings that he termed "'Back to God' Revivals and Healing Campaigns." This was the term he used when his meetings opened at Calvary Temple in Oakland, California, in February of 1950. In much later years, the pastor, V. Ernest Shores, would move to Phoenix First Assembly.

Allen's ministry had, by 1950, developed a clear emphasis on healing. A comparison of newspaper ads around this period suggests that A.A. Allen was emphasizing confirmation of his ministry by what an ad[36] for the Calvary Temple meetings referred to as miracles, healings, and signs and wonders. As the ad expressed it, Allen was a

> Man mightily anointed of God whose ministry is being confirmed by
>
> BIBLE MIRACLES (I Corinthians 12:28)
>
> GIFTS OF HEALING (I Corinthians 12:28)
>
> SIGNS AND WONDERS (Acts 5:12)
>
> One night during the campaign was to be devoted to a "City Wide Holy Ghost Rally."

This emphasis on what were described as "signs and wonders" became a primary thrust of Allen's ministry. Not only did he emphasize supernatural manifestations of the power of God, but throughout his ministry he often represented this as being at odds with organized denominational religion. As early as 1954, Allen spoke of his meetings as encouraging revival and, as he put it,

> This is NOT a revival of forms, ceremonies, rituals, natural ability, talents. It is a revival of POWER, SIGNS, GIFTS, WONDERS![37]

That ad touting "Bible miracles, . . . gifts of healing, . . . and signs and wonders" was dated February 25, 1950. According to another ad around that time,[38] Allen was still holding meetings at Calvary Temple, "Where God is healing the sick. People testify nightly of being healed." Further,

The Power of God Is Moving

Many are saved, delivered from Satan's bondage and filled with the Spirit.

In February of 1950, for example, Allen ministered as a guest evangelist in the fairly small building occupied by the Alton Gospel Tabernacle in Alton, Illinois.[39] A small and unassuming newspaper display ad indicated that Allen would speak at the Sunday morning "worship and communion" service, then again at a Sunday evening evangelistic service.[40] This shows that small churches were still a part of Allen's routine around this time.

Although the venues were still small, the claims of healing were often big. An Oakland woman claimed healing in March 1950 from blood clots on her left leg. By her own testimony,[41]

For five years I had blood clots on my left leg up to the knee. The veins were eaten out to the bottom of the foot, and the doctors declared it would never heal. They tried to graft skin on the limb but it would not grow and my limb was black to my toes.

Her situation was so serious that doctors wanted to amputate, but the woman refused to give them permission. She explained that what she termed "ulcerous sores" in her leg had not only eaten away the veins, but much of the skin as well. Plastic tubes tried to accommodate constantly oozing sores.

At one of A.A. Allen's Oakland meetings, however, Allen prayed for the woman.

After Brother Allen prayed for me, new flesh and skin immediately began to form and grow on the limb. It amazed the doctors. The doctors removed the plastic tubes and sack. Within three days after I was prayed for, my limb was completely covered with new flesh and skin. New flesh even formed where there was no flesh at all.

The *Voice of Healing* magazine observed that after this March 1950 healing, her leg was re-examined when photos were taken in February of 1951. At that time, "only slight discolorations" were visible on her leg. "No soreness has ever returned," the woman noted. "I am completely healed."

By early April of 1950, Allen had moved on to Pampa, Texas, where he was holding yet another "'Back to God' Revival and Healing Campaign." This time it was at another Assemblies of God church, the First Assembly of God, where H.M. Sheats was pastor.

In the meantime, advertising associated with Allen's meetings was becoming more strident. A newspaper display ad for this series of meetings in Pampa declared that Allen's ministry was being confirmed by "Signs following! Miracles of healing! Gifts of the Spirit!" In addition, his meetings were advertised as being "Sound! Biblical!" Prayer for the sick was available nightly, with "scores delivered from tobacco, dope, drink and other habits!"[42]

If another display ad[43] is any indication, by this time momentum was building and audience size was increasing in Allen's meetings in general. "FOLLOW THE CROWDS!" was the ad's top headline. The ad also suggested that these "crowds" should "COME EARLY for a CHOICE SEAT." Allen was still, however, using the "'Back to God' Revival and Healing Campaign" tag.

As he advertised elsewhere during this period, he announced that his ministry was "SCRIPTURALLY SOUND!" and "BIBLICAL!" Presumably this was a reaction against public criticism of healing campaigns in general. Yet, "prayer for the sick" was being offered nightly, and,

> Many Deaf receive hearing instantly. Many Blind receive sight instantly. Goiters, Tumors, Epilepsy, Cancer, all manner of disease and affliction healed instantly.

Further, Allen's ministry was said to be characterized by,

> Hundreds delivered from demon power and unclean spirits, scores delivered from tobacco, dope, drink and other habits.

Even at this early date, Allen appeared to sense a need to justify his ministry emphasis on what were termed signs and wonders of healing. This was not necessarily the norm in small Assemblies of God churches. A.A. Allen was a "Man Mightily Anointed of God," according to a newspaper display ad[44] used to promote a May 1950 series of meetings. This was to be a "'Back to God' Revival and Healing Campaign" at the Assembly of God Church in Covina, California. R.L. Davis was pastor.

Throughout this period, Allen appeared to see a disparity between his signs and wonders emphasis and the normal evangelistic revivals with no such emphasis. Miracles of healing were pointed to as confirmation of his ministry. The ad for the Covina meetings proclaimed that although this would be a healing campaign, Allen's meetings were "Spiritually Sound! Biblical!" In fact, his ministry was "being confirmed," the ad insisted, "by signs following, miracles of healing, [and] gifts of the Spirit."

In Allen's later healing ministry, individuals experienced healing in response to what the New Testament calls the "laying on of hands." Although the 1950 ad could be more clearly worded, it seems to suggest that this was not the case in these meetings. As the ad explained,

ARE YOU SICK OR AFFLICTED?

Allen does not claim to possess the Gifts of Healing . . . never-the-less, hundreds are being healed in his meetings.

Allen does not personally claim to possess a single Gift of the Spirit, yet, in many recent campaigns, night after night, all nine Gifts were in operation, including Miracles and Healings.

Under this man's ministry many are receiving and exercising the Gifts, WITHOUT IMPOSITION OF HANDS OR PROPHETIC UTTERANCE!

In spite of the lack of "imposition of hands," the ad claimed that "scores" were being delivered from "Tobacco, Dope, Drink and Other Habits."

By early November of the same year, A.A. Allen was beginning another of his "'Back to God' Revival and Healing Campaigns," this time in Amarillo. This was at the First Assembly of God Church where E.R. Foster was pastor.

In connection with the Amarillo meetings, a newspaper ad[45] touted "Bible miracles, gifts of healing, signs and wonders." Two services were held daily, with a healing service on Sunday afternoon. "People of all churches" were "invited to bring the sick for prayer," according to the ad.

Allen was ministering in Ada, Oklahoma, in mid-December of 1950. While there, Johnnie Foster, a man whose eye was rendered inoperative by shrapnel during World War II was prayed for by Allen. Foster later testified,

> On "Miracle Night" in A.A. Allen's Salvation-Healing Revival . . . , the Spirit moved in such a mighty way that I realized God was giving me faith to receive vision again. Brother Allen placed his thumb upon my blind eye and prayed. As he prayed, fire seemed to go thru my eye. When he took his thumb away, he commanded me in Jesus' name to see out of that eye. With my hand over my good eye, I opened the eye that had been blind. Immediately I could see the lights in the church and even large print.[46]

He further testified, "My sight continues to get stronger daily."

A new series of Allen meetings began in Oakland, California, on December 31, 1950.[47] This was a "Salvation-Healing Revival" held at the Oakland Revival Tabernacle. Cecil Lowry, who pastored at that facility, reported on the Oakland meetings for the *Voice of Healing*.[48]

Since Allen had been in town the previous year, as Lowry noted, Oakland was familiar with Allen's healing ministry. As Lowry explained,

> Evangelist A.A. Allen did not always lay his hands upon the people who were healed. In fact, he encouraged them from night to night to believe God, and to receive healing, wherever they might be in the Tabernacle.

As a result, according to Lowry,

> Many amazing testimonies were given by those who professed to have received healing in that manner, naming

ruptures, cancers, female disorders, arthritis, tumors, and numerous other afflictions, and glorifying God for complete, fully manifested deliverance.

In addition, Allen reserved each Saturday night for something he termed "Holy Ghost Night." During these meetings, according to Lowry,

> At these services, people throughout the building received the Baptism with the Holy Ghost as they stood praising and glorifying God. There is no way of counting the number who received in this manner during these "receiving services."

Lowry said that the Oakland meetings ended February 12th "in a blaze of glory, with all the balconies filled, and some unable to find seats."

As the end of 1950 neared, the December issue of *The Voice of Healing* magazine[49] listed A.A. Allen meetings in Ada, Oklahoma, scheduled for November 28th through December 17th. These meetings were to be held at the Assembly of God church there. Allen's ministry headquarters address was listed at the time as 1004 S. 14th Street in Lamar, Colorado. This was an address Allen would continue to use for some years.

Chapter 3:

God's Man of Faith and Power

The Voice of Healing was a magazine established by Gordon Lindsay, which promoted a number of healing ministries of the late '40s and the 1950s. The magazine was noting by 1951 that Allen's preaching was being confirmed by "many healings and miracles, scores flocking to the altars for salvation, a great number being delivered from possession and oppression of devils."[50] The same magazine, in an issue dated August 1951, observed that this had been the case "during the past two years." According to the same article in *The Voice of Healing*, these meetings had been conducted "in local churches."

Allen was ministering in Grants Pass, Oregon, in March 1951. A woman who was troubled by "some sort of trouble" in her throat and who attended those meetings said later that her faith "was built up as I heard the preaching and as I read Brother Allen's book." She added,

> The last week of that revival, I asked Brother Allen to pray for my throat. He did, and I believed the work was done. Two days later, on my way to the evening service, I suddenly felt something come loose in my throat. I spit it out. It looked like flesh, light in color, with roots.

Five months later, she said she was "still praising God for complete deliverance from this awful thing."[51]

In the same month that A.A. Allen meetings were being conducted in Grants Pass, a certain J.O. Bryan of Chatham, Louisiana, suffered a stroke. This was accompanied by heightened blood pressure. Bryan was unconscious for four days. When he regained consciousness, he found he had lost his eyesight.

He then learned through one of Allen's radio broadcasts that Allen had scheduled meetings in Tyler, Texas. Bryan's son drove him to Tyler, where Allen insisted that Bryan become born again before receiving prayer for healing. Bryan, according to his own testimony, "promised to make a full surrender to God."

When Allen then prayed for Bryan, he commanded that the spirit of infirmity leave: "Thou spirit of infirmity, thou who makes this man blind, I bind and rebuke you now in the name of Jesus! I command you in Jesus' name to go now!"

Allen had his thumbs over Bryan's eyes. Before removing his hand, he told Bryan, "My friend, in Jesus' name, in the power of the Spirit, I command you to open your eyes and see normally this minute!" Bryan later testified that the moment Allen removed his hand, he was instantly able to see. He said that he was able to see perfectly.[52]

Allen scheduled meetings for May 1st in Salem, Oregon, to be followed by meetings in Stockton, California in June and in Modesto in July. Then he would move on to Atlanta, Georgia, where he was scheduled to minister August 26th.[53]

These meetings evidently would come to mark the end of A.A. Allen's dependence on Assemblies of God church buildings. Suggestions have been made in recent years that seem to imply that Allen first ventured into holding tent crusades in 1956, when he purchased the tent that had been owned by recently deceased fellow minister Jack Coe.[54] This was not the case, however.

Instead, Allen had purchased a tent by 1951, and it appears to have been used by the time of Allen meetings scheduled to begin on the 4th of July in 1951 in Yakima, Washington.[55] The Yakima revival was described as a "union tent meeting" held at the fair grounds.[56]

According to Paul Cunningham, who later worked with Allen, Allen's ministry simply eventually outgrew available church buildings. According to Cunningham, his wife urged him to remain associated with the Assemblies of God, but he declared that he could not. The reason, according to Allen, was that none of the Assemblies of God church buildings at the time were large enough to house his revivals.[57]

Already by the summer of 1951, Allen was beginning to venture out into conducting "union revivals." This meant that instead of holding a meeting for one specific church and using its facilities, Allen was now beginning to hold larger tent revivals, while seeking the aid and assistance of local congregations. "A 100 x 200 foot tent has been made available," the *Voice of*

Healing noted, "and this enlarged ministry is scheduled to begin in Yakima, Washington, at the Fair Grounds on July 4th" in 1951.[58]

The July 1951 issue of *The Voice of Healing* included a "Special Notice" from A.A. Allen. That notice was used to announce to the public that Allen had just obtained a huge tent:

A SPECIAL NOTICE BY A.A. ALLEN

Evangelist A.A. Allen wishes to announce that he has just secured a large tent seating several thousand. Not knowing ahead of time that he would be able to secure these facilities, he has open dates for a few tent campaigns. Those interested write him immediately, 1004 S. 14th St., Lamar, Colorado.

The reason for this shift from the use of church buildings to tents, according *The Voice of Healing*, was because of tremendous moves during the past two years. As the magazine expressed it,

God has blessed and honored the faithful preaching of His word, by confirming the Word with many healings and miracles, scores flocking to the altars for salvation, a great number being delivered from possession and oppression of devils in A.A. Allen's meetings during the past two years.

Around this time, Gordon Kampfer, a Eugene, Oregon minister, decided to resign as pastor in order to travel with Allen. His wife intended to play the organ.[59] Kampfer was pastor of the Assembly of God Church at 710 13th Avenue West in Eugene.[60] Earlier, in 1943, he had pastored the South Bend Assembly of God in South Bend, Washington.[61]

A 1949 newspaper article discussed an upcoming sermon by Kampfer at the Assembly of God church. His topic was to be "Hell - at Any Price." "These are days," according to Kampfer, "when people are questioning the plain truths of God's Word concerning judgment, the hereafter, and the existence of a place of everlasting punishment." This evening message was to be preceded by a morning sermon titled "Sowing and Reaping."[62]

As already mentioned, the 1951 Yakima tent revival with A.A. Allen was said to be a "union meeting" being sponsored by multiple "Full Gospel" churches in the Yakima Valley.[63] The Yakima meetings seem to have epitomized a period of major change in Allen's ministry.

A minister named B.V. Jones was appointed "chairman" of the Yakima meetings, and he later reported on them for *The Voice of Healing*:[64]

> "Of all the revival meetings we have attended, this has been the greatest outpouring and visitation of the old-time power of Pentecost we have ever witnessed," declared many of the ministers and those attending the A.A. Allen Valley-wide union tent revival.

According to Jones, the Allen tent revival brought together ministers of several denominations as they worked together, especially to minister salvation:

> Denominational lines were forgotten as ministers of the Assemblies of God, Pentecostal holiness, Church of God, and other Full Gospel organizations, as well as independent groups, worked and prayed side by side for the salvation of the lost and the deliverance of those oppressed by the enemy.

It was impossible to keep a count of the number seeking salvation . . . . There were many nights when over one hundred answered the call. The greatest night of the campaign was when over two hundred answered the call, overflowing the two prayer tents.

In fact, according to Jones,

Conviction was so heavy on the sinners that there were nights when they came running and even screaming to the altars.

He noted that various individuals said regarding the Allen revival, "This is just what we have been praying for for years."

The Yakima crusade was the scene of notable reported healings. A 12-year old boy testified to healing at Yakima of an eardrum which a doctor said had burst. According to his mother, the healing was instantaneous. She said that "He heard even the faintest sounds with the ear the doctor said would never hear again."[65]

Another individual who said that a cancer had spread on her hand and was "very bad." For the next several days after Allen prayed for her, however, according to her testimony, the cancer "began to dry up:"

As it withered, it loosened and came out by the roots, leaving ugly holes where the roots had been. These holes gradually filled in and smoothed over with new flesh.

It has now been three months since I was healed. My hand is as smooth as a child's and only a small scar remains. No pain has ever returned.[66]

A man attending the Yakima meetings also complained of a cancer on his face, near his right eye. "It caused me much anxiety and pain," he said. Three days after Allen prayed for him, according to the man,

> the Spirit of the Lord came upon me in an unusual way. I realized that something was taking place as the cancer began to tingle. Suddenly the cancer vanished! I could never find it. It just disappeared.

He said that, "Even the skin where the cancer had been was smooth and no discoloration was left." Three months later, he was still free from cancer.[67]

According to B.V. Jones, chairman of the Yakima meetings,

> How our faith was inspired as we witnessed the lame walking, the deaf hearing and all manner of sickness healed. Demon oppression was broken and many who had been in bondage and torment found joy and victory.

For Allen's ministry, the Yakima meetings seemed to mark a major move forward. For B.V. Jones, the Allen meetings in Yakima were a boon to his own church. "Many" of his congregation, he said, had been healed, and Sunday School attendance, which seems to have in those days served as a benchmark by which to measure church size, was up 40%. Jones claimed that he even needed to hire a new assistant pastor to deal with his new members. Jones also explained that,

> In the Sunday night offerings, people from the local churches were given opportunity to support their own local church. Again and again Brother Allen urged the people to be faithful in supporting the local churches

with their tithes and offerings, as well as by their faithful attendance after the revival was closed. No distressing "pulls" were made for finances for the campaign, yet God supplied every need.

The Yakima revival concluded with a special baptismal service. Ministers representing the local churches that had supported Allen's meetings performed water baptisms in the tent's "portable canvas baptismal pool." "The sound scriptural ministry and methods of Brother Allen," according to B.V. Jones, "did much to break down prejudice toward this type of ministry."

Allen then set up his tent on a Highway 30 near the high school in Nampa, Idaho for meetings scheduled for August 15th through September 9th.[68] Reported healings included that of a young woman who found she was able to remove a back brace she had worn after a car accident.

In addition, a baby was healed of what was described as a "bad rupture." A cooperating local pastor said that "the high point" was a water baptismal service in which more than a hundred persons were baptized in a "portable baptistry" that had been set up in the tent. Even though "some" arrived at Allen's Nampa meetings in a critical state, they were said to have "immediately recognized the sanction of the Holy Ghost upon the great ministry . . . . "[69]

By this time, A.A. Allen was issuing "prayer cloths" for healing, which were sent by mail to those requesting them. Prayer cloths have been, and still are, used by a number of ministries with a belief in healing. This practice is generally tied to a passage of scripture, Acts 19:11-12.

In that passage, the apostle Paul was in Ephesus, on the west coast of what is now Turkey. Paul had attempted to teach in the local synagogue. When he was barred from that venue, however, he moved his instruction to the "school of one Tyrannus," where he taught for two years. Acts 19:11-12 then continues:

> And God worked special miracles by the hands of Paul, so that from his body were brought to the sick handkerchiefs or aprons, and the diseases departed from them and the evil spirits went out of them.

Late in 1951, a woman had been bothered by a rapidly expanding growth on her face. A doctor wanted to remove it and have it analyzed, but instead she wrote to Allen for a prayer cloth. As she phrased it, ". . . I did not keep the appointment, but decided to trust God." In her words, "I placed the cloth on the growth, and now, praise God, it is gone."[70]

As 1951 closed, the organization associated with *The Voice of Healing* (TVH) magazine held a three-day conference. This conference, which featured big name healing evangelists ministering to a crowd of about 2,500, was held December 11-13 in the Tulsa Convention Hall. The final message on the final day was brought by A.A. Allen, described as a "veteran of TVH fellowship." Allen delivered what was termed a "fiery sermon on the power of the gifts of the Spirit in their proper operation."[71]

Regarding such gifts, an undated flyer asserts the claim that "Under Allen's ministry many are receiving and exercising 'gifts' without imposition of hands or prophetic utterance!"[72]

A man testified that as a result of Allen's ministry in St. Petersburg, Florida, on January 15, 1952, he was healed of a hernia. Not only that, but he said that, "As he prayed, I could feel the hernia moving." He added that every trace of the problem was gone by the next morning. Three and a half months later, he said that no sign of the problem had returned.[73]

Later in 1952, Allen set up his tent in Galveston, Texas, holding what a local paper called "the A.A. Allen Salvation-Healing Revival."[74] In contrast to later Allen meetings, which seemed to often attract criticism and controversy, this still-early Allen revival was described in a local paper as simply including meetings "especially planned for the benefit of the sick, suffering, and afflicted."

This was in addition to prayer for those in need of healing in each evening service, which were scheduled to begin at 7:30. Gordon Kampfer was Allen's musical director and business manager at the time. Kampfer's wife served as organist. Allen was also said to have "a large staff" who took care of "tent maintenance and office duties."[75]

Some of Allen's upcoming "prophetic sermon topics" were announced. These were said to include "God's Last Message to a Dying World," "Has the World Already Passed God's Last Sign Post?" "Nearing Armageddon," "World War Number Three in Prophecy," "Will Russia Win the Atom Bomb Race?" "Stalin's Funeral," and "The Man Whose Number is 666."

The latter was also the title of one of Allen's many books and booklets which were published and distributed by his ministry. The booklet titled *The Man Whose Number is 666!* is dated 1953,[76] right around the time that Allen was actually ministering this sermon in his revival crusades. This title was sold in Allen's meetings for 50 cents.

The booklet's cover asks the question, "Will you receive the mark of this coming World Dictator?" Although Allen pointed out that a number of other ministers had advanced a variety of theories as to who would be the "beast" of the book of Revelation, the "man whose number is 666," he chose to decline to give his opinion on the matter.

"Although I do have my own idea who this great personality will be, it is not my plan in this booklet to name this beast," he said. Allen did note, however, that God gave him a message regarding this individual:

> That message is far greater than a personality, or a man, or a name! The real message of God through Revelation 13 is a warning to the people of my day that this man - whatever his name may be - is a MAN RAISED UP BY THE DEVIL, empowered by the devil, placed upon the seat of authority by the devil! Whether he comes to power through the United Nations Organization or by popular vote, this is THE DEVIL'S MAN, raised up by the devil himself, to carry out the devil's plans during the tribulation period![77]

A newspaper ad which publicized various Allen "prophetic sermon topics" including the matter of the mark of the beast also mentioned his sermon titled "God's Last Message to a Dying World." This sermon was also published in booklet form around the same time, and also sold for 50 cents.

According to an ad promoting the booklet, it contained "amazing scientific information" designed to convince the reader that "the world is sick, on its death bed, dying right now!"

World's greatest scientists say:

> "Only a miracle of God saved the world from entire disintegration when the U. S. exploded the last 'H' bomb" (This has been a close secret)

"New bacteriological weapons could kill all living things in six hours"

"The world's time clock reads three minutes till midnight, the time left before all civilization will come to an end"

"The new 'G' gas could kill millions in seconds"[78]

This booklet epitomized a tendency for Allen to, at times, use events of the day and information from popular news articles as a basis for controversial sermons pertaining to the "end times."

Gordon Kampfer was still described as a ministry associate of Allen as late as August 1954. In that month, Kampfer was lauded as "a man of deep, sincere conviction, and a soldier of the old paths." He was further described as "a contender for the faith that was once delivered unto the saints."[79]

The man making those statements was Hansel P. Vibbert, an Assemblies of God pastor in Evansville, Indiana. Vibbert claimed in 1954 that sponsoring Allen meetings had been key to the growth of his own church.

Pastors often refer to the number of those in Sunday School as a true indicator of the size of church attendance. Vibbert said he had just a hundred in Sunday school when he first met Allen six years earlier, or about 1948. The first service Vibbert held with Allen as guest minister was in 1949.[80]

"Brother Allen's meetings here have been great stepping-stairs in our program for the Lord," said Vibbert. "We are soon to begin construction on a great tabernacle that will seat 3,000."[81] He also noted that his church had been "revolutionized" as they "received the light on tithing" through Allen's teaching.

Vibbert added that Allen preached "a sound gospel good for any church." Vibbert further explained his involvement with Allen's ministry:

One of the outstanding memories in my mind of A.A. Allen was his prayer life during that meeting, as he stayed with us in a small apartment we had over the church. I told my wife after the revival that the day would come, should Jesus tarry, that A.A. Allen, because of his consecration, would preach to tens of thousands, and I have seen it come to pass. After an association of six years and working in his great meetings, I will back him as one of God's greatest soul winners alive today.[82]

A woman who said she had been suffering from cerebral hemorrhage with complete paralysis, plus an inability to speak, claimed healing as a result of the Galveston meetings. Well known minister James W. Drush, who was pastor of the church the woman attended, said that he witnessed her healing, along with "hundreds of people."[83]

Allen began a "Salvation Healing Revival" in Havana, Cuba, on February 15, 1952. The location was on a heavily traveled street in the heart of the city.[84] A publicity photo in June showed the look of "elation" on the face of a man said to have been healed in the Havana meetings from a condition described as having been "stone blind."[85]

Another look of "elation" was said to be evident when a man was able to hear after having been deaf for 14 years. He was quoted as saying,

The first night I attended I saw immediately it was different than anything I had ever seen, but I liked what the man said from the Bible, and when I saw so many being healed, I went up. Now I can hear everything.[86]

A Havana woman had been looking to idols and images for deliverance from a paralyzed condition, but to no avail. When she testified to complete healing, she gave all her idols and images, including one of St. Lazarus, "the 'healing saint,'" to add to what was referred to as "Bro. Allen's collection."[87] In at least one of his TV programs, Allen showed a statue of Lazarus and other icons which had prayed to by individuals before attending Allen's meetings, then discarded.

In another case, a certain Allen Hurdle of Havana said that he had been afflicted for months with what was termed a "strange affliction" which came on him "suddenly while committing sin." After months of excruciating pain, the hospital sent him home to die. Friends made a bed for him in a car so that he could be transported to Allen's meetings. When he arrived, his screams of pain were so extreme that a policeman came, who was said to have thought Hurdle was being murdered.

Allen came to the car where Hurdle was lying, in order to pray for him. Hurdle testified later,

> When Allen finally came to the car to pray for me, he looked at the medal of Saint Christopher, which was supposed to protect me from harm, sickness and accident and asked: "If this medal is supposed to protect you from all these things, why do I read on the back side IN CASE OF ACCIDENT OR SICKNESS CALL A PRIEST?"

When Allen prayed, the pain left so suddenly, according to Hurdle's testimony, that he was "amazed." He sat up, got out of the car, and testified to being "well ever since."[88]

Another series of Allen tent meetings closed in Lakeland, Florida on April 13th, 1952. A.A. Allen offered a prayer for those who wanted "special faith" for healing:

> Allen made a short exhortation on faith and declared that Christ was the Author and Finisher of our faith and that it is also given as a gift as well as a fruit. Hundreds stood as Allen prayed[,] asking God to remove every hindrance to faith and give the people faith.

A number of people who believed they had received, then remained standing, while Allen prayed that healing would be manifested. Many then testified to immediate healing. These included a woman who removed bandages from "her limb" which had been bandaged "for six years with ulcerous sores."[89]

A Baptist minister by the name of John A. Mitchell said that during Allen's meetings in both Lakeland and St. Petersburg, Florida, he personally investigated the healings that were claimed in Allen's tent. He claimed that he had found them to be genuine:

> Many nights when Rev. Allen prayed for the sick, I stood at the front with numerous other ministers and personally witnessed people being healed! Many of the cases I personally investigated and also interviewed doctors and nurses who attended these sick people that were healed and found the healings to be authentic.

Mitchell also said that during one of the meetings he attended, a man with a "large, cruel cancer on his face" experienced having that cancer simply drop from his face.[90] This sounds reminiscent of the ministry of Jack Coe, another well-known tent-based healing evangelist of the era. Coe, in one of his televised healing services, prayed for a woman with a cancer on her face, then simply pulled the cancer off with his fingers.

May of 1952 saw Allen's team pitching their tent in Greenville, Mississippi. Although, at least in later years, the A.A. Allen ministry would be known for its emphasis on racial integration, a newspaper display ad appearing on May 23, 1952 for the Greenville meetings noted in parentheses, at the bottom of the ad, "(SPECIAL RESERVED SECTION FOR COLORED)."[91] The ad, of course, does not provide insight as to whether this statement was inserted due to local pressure, or in order to ensure heavy attendance by whites.

That ad emphasized a sermon topic that had been promoted in Galveston, that being "Stalin's Funeral." In Allen's characteristically provocative style, the sermon was promoted in spectacular terms. The audience was urged to picture dramatic and recent events:

Hear this great lecturer Friday Night, 7:30 (May 30)

Hear Stalin's funeral preached! See the casket! All Communists urged to attend! Know what is ahead for Russia![92]

This was preceded by another timely message on the 23rd, again capitalizing on issues in the news. The topic, as already featured elsewhere, was "Will Russia Win the Atom Bomb Race?" Unlike the "Stalin's Funeral" message, where "All Communists" were urged to attend, for this earlier message, no Communists were to be admitted:

No Communists allowed on this night! Admittance by ticket only. Tickets given free at Main Entrance of tent to all who pledge they are not Communists. [93]

One of those testifying to healing when Allen ministered in Greenville, Mississippi said that she received her healing on May 25, 1952. She said that 11 years earlier, a nerve in her foot was severed as the result of an accident. Her leg from the hip down became paralyzed several years later. When Allen prayed for her, according to her testimony, life returned to her foot instantly.[94]

A feature of the Greenville meetings was "Deliverance Nights." This was when many testified to having been set free from "oppressing, tormenting spirits" as the result of entering "special prayer lines." Although some locals had expressed skepticism that Allen could fill his tent in such a small town, the tent was described as "packed" by the first Sunday. On the final night of the Greenville meetings, about 2,000 had to stand outside the perimeter of the tent because of lack of space inside.[95]

Louisville, Kentucky, was another ministry destination for A.A. Allen in 1952, with meetings closing there on June 30th. One memorable moment was said to have been when a man who testified to healing pushed Allen in the wheelchair that the man had himself occupied a few moments before. Another individual claimed that he experienced instantaneous healing from a serious back and hip injury.[96]

A Move into Radio

Despite his 1949 squabble with his Corpus Christi church over starting a radio ministry, Allen doesn't appear to have made his first purchase of radio time until 1953.[97] Soon after he made this move, the ministry of A.A. Allen was being heard on radio stations across the United States and in Mexico and Cuba as the *Allen Revival Hour.*

By 1953, the Allen Revival Hour was being carried on seven stations. A list includes American cities alongside the stations' call letters. A look at the call letters themselves, however, reveals that three of the seven - XEG, XELO, and XEDM - were stations based in Mexico.[98]

By October of 1954, the list had grown to include 14 stations, with one more Mexican station being added: XERF, based in Ciudad Acuña, Coahuila, but with offices in Del Rio, Texas. An earlier unrelated station in the same town was the legendary "border blaster" made famous by renowned medical quack John R. Brinkley.

In addition to Allen's regular 15-minute radio program, *The Allen Revival Hour*, a 30-minute program called *The Hour of Deliverance* was being aired in Cuba as a "missionary project" outreach of *The Allen Revival Hour*. The program in Cuba was aired in Spanish, and by August of 1954 was carried over 11 stations in Cuba.[99] Allen's organization sought in 1954 to expand the outreach into other Spanish-speaking countries.[100] A symbiotic relationship was doubtless in operation between Allen's Spanish-language broadcasts in Cuba and his healing and deliverance meetings in that country.[101]

Two years after Allen's radio broadcasts began, a 1955 newspaper ad for Allen's ministry[102] listed four stations on which San Antonio residents could hear Allen. Two of those stations - XEG and XELO - were based in Mexico. In October of that same year, the inaugural issue of Allen's *Miracle Magazine* appeared, with a listing of 16 U.S. radio stations, plus XEG and XELO, airing the *Allen Revival Hour*.[103]

Today, XEG is known as La Ranchera de Monterrey. At night, this high-power AM blaster from Nuevo León, Mexico, can be heard as far north as the Midwestern United States. By 1950, XEG was selling time through an American sales rep. At least three different Mexican stations have, over the years, used the XELO call letters. Allen's involvement was probably while the station was located in Juarez, since XELO appears to have moved there from Tijuana by the early 1950s.[104]

In 1953, Allen was also using XEDM. "These super-power stations," as he put it, which were located "across the Mexican border" were capable of reaching "all forty-eight states and Canada, Alaska, Mexico, New Zealand, Bahamas, Cuba, British Guiana, and other parts of the western hemisphere."[105]

These stations were known as "border blasters" because they were powerful. These Mexican AM stations were equipped to penetrate the United States airwaves while avoiding more restrictive U.S. broadcast regulation.

The border blaster movement, if it could be called that, seems to have originated when an American broadcaster with dubious medical credentials was forced off of U.S. radio and wanted to continue his lucrative medical practice via radio. That was John R. Brinkley, known for promoting his surgery which involved implanting goat testicular tissue in adult men in an attempt to cure impotence.

Lexie Allen, in her biography of her husband A.A. Allen, quotes from a typical opening used in Allen's radio broadcasts:

God's man of faith and power is on the air! From coast to coast, under one of the world's largest gospel tents, this man with a supernatural ministry is leading thousands to Christ. Thousands are healed and delivered, as Allen prays the prayer of faith, for the sick and suffering.

Here, now, is Evangelist A.A. Allen, the man whom God has sent to bring deliverance to you![106]

Deliverance from evil spirits, as well as healing from physical ailments and infirmities, were both hallmarks of Allen's ministry from its early days until his death in 1970. Seemingly countless "healing evangelists" erected tents which dotted the American landscape in the late 1940s and throughout the 1950s and '60s. Not all of them emphasized deliverance, however. Deliverance was a primary aspect of Allen's ministry.

Deliverance was the subject of *Deliver Me*, an undated booklet by Allen and published by his ministry. "Never has there been a time when so many thousands confessed their need of deliverance," Allen noted in the foreword. The booklet did not just discuss deliverance in the more customary sense, however. In its pages, Allen also taught on "Deliverance from Powerless Form" in the churches, "Deliverance from Unscriptural Religious Influence," and "Deliverance from Unscriptural Church Government."

What Allen had in mind by referring to "powerless form" is explained in his text. There Allen said that many are kept in bondage by religious spirits:

> It may be a religious demon. His special job is to lead you away from the Bible and let you have mere form and ceremony and ritual instead of the old-fashioned power of the Holy Ghost and old-fashioned revival. . . .

> God wants you to get away from your form and your ceremony and ritual and once more worship Him in spirit and in truth. He wants you to get lost in God until your spirit meets him, and then something is going to happen.[107]

A.A. Allen picked up on the deliverance theme in what he called "A Personal Message to my Radio Friends" in a special 1953 promotional publication.[108] He pointed out that the Soviet Union was threatening the United States with nuclear annihilation, but that an invasion of a different sort had already begun.

An invasion of demonic forces, according to Allen, had already begun and was oppressing men and women "physically, mentally, and spiritually." In his television programs, Allen frequently treated psychological issues, including stress, worry, and depression, as demonic forces which could be dealt with by spiritual means.

"Already," noted Allen, the effects of this invasion were evident in mental institutions, jails, courts, hospitals, and cemeteries. He spoke of demons of lust ("and lust is a demon," Allen said), demons of suicide, and "tormenting demons of fear (worry)" that led to premature death.[109]

In 1953, Allen held a "City-Wide Union Tent Meeting" in Houston from April 1st through the 26th, followed by another "City-Wide Union Tent Meeting" from April 30th through May 24th, this time in Beaumont, Texas.[110]

By early September, A.A. Allen had moved on to Evansville, Indiana, where he had scheduled a City-Wide Tent Meeting for September 2-27. Hansel Vibbert, discussed earlier, was Allen's contact person for the Evansville meetings. The weather reached below freezing temperatures, but the tent was heated and, according to Vibbert, "packed to the side walls."[111]

At one point during the Evansville meetings, a man received healing for a leg which required a brace. Allen advised the man to take the brace off, but he replied that he could not, because it required a screwdriver.

Just then, his wife, who was seated a great distance from the platform, stood up and shouted "I have the screwdriver!" According to Vibbert, she had brought the screwdriver in faith. When the brace was removed, the man found that he could walk.[112]

After the meetings in Evansville, Indiana, it was then on to Corpus Christ, Texas for another City Wide Tent Meeting, October 7 through November 1.[113] This was followed by an appearance of Allen at the 5th annual Voice of Healing Convention in Chicago, scheduled for December 8-11, 1953.[114]

The Move to Dallas

In order to promote and share information regarding the healing campaigns of William Branham, Gordon Lindsay established a magazine in 1948 titled *The Voice of Healing*. Before long, the magazine would be used in order to spread the word about the ministry activities of what seemed to be an ever-growing number of healing evangelists.

A.A. Allen's address was dutifully recorded in each issue of the magazine from at least December 1950 through December 1953. That address remained constant during that period, and was always publicized as 1004 South 14th Street, Lamar, Colorado. When 1954 began, however, the first issue of the new year, the January 1954, showed that Allen had moved his ministry headquarters from Lamar, Colorado, to a new address: P.O. Box 8595, Dallas, Texas.

Then, for the next several years, A.A. Allen and his family would live in Dallas, where they attended Oak Cliff Assembly of God. As one of Allen's employees, David Hollis, remembers, however, the Allens were rarely in town. Instead, they were usually engaged in ministry elsewhere.[115]

Hollis recalls that the staff size was, at the time, somewhere around 20. Allen found that Hollis was mechanically inclined and capable of repairing the equipment then in use for maintaining a mailing list and handling items to be mailed.

As a result, Allen canceled contracts with outside companies and put Hollis in charge of that facet of his ministry. This enabled Hollis to start his own business which entailed setting up offices and office equipment for a number of other ministries. This included those of such well known figures as Jack Coe and, eventually, Benny Hinn.

Allen's choice of Oak Cliff Assembly of God as a home church seems, in retrospect, particularly apt. Oak Cliff's pastor was H.C. Noah, widely known for his support of the healing ministry in general and the Voice of Healing movement in particular.

Shortly before Allen's move to Dallas, Noah wrote an article for *The Voice of Healing* magazine in which he emphasized the vital significance of the healing ministry for his church and congregation.[116] In fact, Noah listed some of those in the healing ministry who had visited Oak Cliff or who had ministered in campaigns in association with the assembly. That list includes some of the most significant healing ministers of the Voice of Healing era:

A series of Salvation and Divine Healing campaigns averaging about six weeks each have lighted a fire that burns brightly and continuously in this church. During the last four years the following have held meetings here in the order named: Evangelists Jack Coe, Oral Roberts, Mildred Wicks, A.A. Allen, O.L. Jaggers, Charles Dobbins, Gayle Jackson, . . . , W.V. Grant, Paul Cain, ...[117]

Noah described how he became involved in healing revival meetings. He spoke of a profound personal experience with God during meetings with healing evangelist Jack Coe. Then, he said,

> The Divine river was flowing. I was now ready to venture. I was now a desperate man. This led to the sponsoring of healing meetings. The first one was city-wide, by Oral Roberts.

He said that such meetings were continuing to set "our church on fire."[118]

Beginning in 1954, H. Kent Rogers became associated with Allen's ministry. At the time of Allen's death in 1970, Rogers was president of A.A. Allen Revivals, Inc.[119]

During the summer of 1954, the *Los Angeles Times* noted that "Summertime is evangelism time." As a result, "Big brown tents, each capable of holding a three-ring circus," were dotting the landscape across Southern California.[120]

Among those who erected such tents was A.A. Allen, who drove stakes in El Monte, near L.A., in July. Allen was noted at the time as leaning toward "the revelation-healing phrases of his profession." One local pastor declared of the Allen crusade in El Monte, "Allen Revival? God's Revival! Bible days are here again!"[121] *The Voice of Healing* magazine noted that in one particular Allen service, which was designated "Holy Ghost Night," 2,500 people "marched over the ramp" in order to receive the Holy Spirit.[122]

Around the same time, the L.A. area was the location for revival crusades by other big-name evangelists, including William Branham and Tommy Hicks. At the time, there seemed to be "no shortage of revivalists:"

Although the great pre-radio, pre-movie evangelism days of Gypsy Smith and others are over, there is no shortage of revivalists in these times, and a few of them exert an influence over large numbers of people.[123]

While in El Monte, Allen planned for a special "Liberation Week," while declaring that "hundreds are fasting and praying for your deliverance." He claimed that demons were binding "millions" but that these could expect deliverance via "today's authority on demonology."[124]

Deliverance from demons was certainly being touted by this time as a central feature of Allen's ministry. Gordon Lindsay, editor of *The Voice of Healing* magazine, summed up a Voice of Healing convention in the final issue for 1954:

Wednesday night the huge auditorium was almost filled. Evangelist A.A. Allen delivered a powerful message on demonology, on which he has come to be recognized as an authority.

This indicates that by this time, an emphasis on deliverance was increasingly being associated with Allen's ministry.

Lindsay indicated what types of demon activity Allen had in mind. He said that Allen began his sermon by asserting that he was, as Lindsay put it, "a son of God" and "not afraid of the devil." Further, Gordon Lindsay said that Allen was there to "break the fetters of those who were bound and to set the captives free." Lindsay further described Allen's deliverance ministry:

He said eight out of ten people in America are possessed or oppressed by demon spirits. He pointed out that there are an estimated 8,000,000 homosexuals in America. He said 67,000,000 cannot sleep at night. He startled many by telling how demons have talked through their victims at various times in his meetings when he had proceeded to cast them out.

Lindsay added that "hundreds rushed back stage to be delivered" since room in front of the stage could not hold the crowds.[125]

A frequent theme in Allen's spoken messages was that countless Americans are vexed with nervous or psychological conditions that are the result of demon activity. In referring to Allen services in 1954, *The Voice of Healing* magazine noted that "In the great liberation services in the Allen campaigns, thousands are set free from demon power, lust, fear, worry, etc."[126]

A.A. Allen connected individuals' unusual struggles with sin and psychological bondages to be demon-related. "Liberation Nights" were established for the purpose of "exposing the activity of demons in the world today" as well as offering prayer for those who were identified as "possessed, oppressed, or vexed by demons."[127]

By late 1954, Allen meetings were sometimes characterized by demonstrations of deliverance involving demons speaking through people. As Allen himself noted in connection with a series of meetings held late in 1954,

> Thousands have attended these meetings the last two weeks, and have declared that although they had heard many sermons on the subject of demon possession, and had seen many of these people prayed for, THIS WAS THE FIRST TIME THEY HAD ACTUALLY WITNESSED DEMONS COMING OUT AND HEARD DEMONS TALK. In many cases, the demon

actually used the person's lips and talked, saying "I WON'T COME OUT."[128]

By early 1955, the ministry of A.A. Allen had become solidly united with the Voice of Healing movement led by Gordon Lindsay. As a part of its "Billion Souls Crusade," Allen was cooperating in huge meetings with the likes of evangelists T. L. Osborn and Velmer Gardner.

The "Billion Souls Crusade" appears to have been a Gordon Lindsay creation. He explained that it represented not an attempt to convert a billion individuals, but to reach a billion with the Gospel message:

> We desire again to make clear the meaning of THE BILLION SOULS CRUSADE. The Bible does not teach that all who hear will accept the Gospel. What the term expresses is that there are a billion and more souls who have not been evangelized, but who will listen to the Gospel, if it is preached "with the signs following."[129]

Allen found camaraderie and similarity of purpose in the goals and activities of the Voice of Healing movement, especially the part about the "signs following." He pointed to one of Osborn's films, termed missionary films, as demonstrating the viability and even necessity of what Allen termed "signs, wonders and miracles:"

> Osborn's film, "Java Harvest" filmed in Indonesia during his great campaign there, is bringing before the people EVIDENCE that the only way to reach and convert the heathen is with this Gospel of SIGNS, WONDERS AND MIRACLES.[130]

Around this time, Allen was growing increasingly impatient with the limitations of denominational religion. By later that same year, 1955, events would propel him out of denominational circles forever, and even beyond the confines of the Voice of Healing organization.

But for the time being, Allen saw a kindred spirit among the "healing evangelists" affiliated with the Voice of Healing movement and with its magazine, designed to promote affiliate ministers' healing meetings. Allen spoke in glowing terms of the efforts of Gordon Lindsay as editor of *The Voice of Healing*:

> Gordon Lindsay's great sermon on "Crusade for World Fellowship" is being so blessed of the Lord that ministers of all denominations are breaking down denominational barriers and rolling up sectarian lines and are joining hands one with one another with the conviction, "we be brethren" and "we be all members of the same body."

He further emphasized the failings of the organized denominations:

> As for my part in these great rallies, I wish to emphasize that up until today the great commission "GO YE" is still unfulfilled. The devil knows it is the truth that will set the people free and in these rallies we are presenting only facts that will stir the people to action. Few people in our churches realize that in the last generation the church let 750 million heathen slip through her fingers into eternity without God![131]

Also around this time, Allen was doing a brisk business, as were some of his colleagues in the healing revival movement. Evangelist W. V. Grant in particular issued numerous books, booklets actually, which appeared to be transcripts of his sermons. Many were issued using his "Faith Clinic" organizational name, based in Dallas.

1955: A Pivotal Year

Allen's book ministry would be supplemented, however, by what would eventually become a widely circulated magazine, his own *Miracle Magazine*. *Miracle Magazine* was to emerge later this same year — 1955, a year which proved to be a pivotal year in the ministry of A.A. Allen.

This would be the year in which Allen would truly strike out on his own, blazing his own path in ministry that would not be dependent on anyone else. The rift with his denomination and even with the Voice of Healing movement was inevitable.

His wife Lexie was still with him. His relationship with her would become the basis for yet another rift, but for now he was still selling her account of his life, a book she authored which was titled *God's Man of Faith and Power*.

After their eventual divorce, Allen would pen his own account, titled *Born to Lose, Bound to Win*. According to Paul J. Cunningham, who worked closely with Allen, the new volume would be a chance for A.A. Allen to tell his own story his own way, rather than through his wife's vantage point.[132]

In the meantime, however, ads in 1955, promoting Lexie's book about her husband, proclaimed that "You'll THRILL to every WORD of this heart-gripping STORY!":

Read of his childhood in a drunkard's home, torn by strife and jealousy; young manhood spent in riotous living, converted and called to preach in early twenties; a struggling pastor in pioneer fields; then the transforming experience that empowered him to blaze a trail of Holy Ghost revival across America!"[133]

Another publication promoted in similarly glowing terms at the same time was *Miracles Today*, a book that used the same title as Allen's TV program. Not just did it describe healings evident in the Allen crusades, but promotions declared that "*EACH PAGE PULSATES* WITH 'BOOK-OF-ACTS POWER!'"[134]

A 1955 ministry promotion encouraged the masses to "FOLLOW THE CROWD."[135] "Will Russia win the A-bomb race?'" was asked by the same promotion, which announced "No Communists allowed on this night!" The ad was used in order to promote the A.A. Allen "salvation, Holy Ghost healing revival" to be held in what was called the "big tent" erected for that purpose on South Presa Street in San Antonio. Today, that location is slightly west of the confluence of Interstates 10 and 37 in the south part of town.

This was during the height of the Cold War. Just a year earlier, an estimated 20 million viewers had watched the Army-McCarthy hearings, which opened on April 22, 1954. Although popular support for Senator Joseph McCarthy, noted for his accusatory tactics directed toward supposed Communists, plummeted during the hearings, a strong anti-Soviet sentiment persisted. In fact, just five years after Allen's ad appeared, Soviet premier Nikita Krushchev would boast that the presence of Soviet ICBMs was causing "Main Street Americans" to "shake from fear for the first time in their lives."[136]

No one was to be admitted without first obtaining a free ticket given only to those who would "pledge they are not Communists!" The ad suggested that those who make the pledge should come early in order to ensure getting a good seat.

Perhaps some sort of connection was being implied by the same ad's promotion of yet another Allen message, which similarly related current events to Biblical prophecies in a provocative way. That message was titled "The Man Whose Number if 666." "Who is this man who soon put his brand on you?" the advertisement asked, while adding "Don't miss this! Amazing! Startling! Dynamic!"

At a time when denominational affiliation prevailed to, assumedly, a much greater degree than today, the ad proclaimed in two large headlines that Allen's meetings were suitable for those of any religious persuasion. "Thousands are attending. For all people of all churches," was headlined near the top of the ad. The bottom of the same ad noted, in large capitals, that the revival was "FOR ALL PEOPLE OF ALL CHURCHES."

In addition, Allen, referred to as "today's authority on demonology," would be preaching on "Demon Power and How to Be Free." A list of seven types of demons, with an explanation of how "these demons bind millions today" also appeared. Two services daily were announced, with a 7 p.m. "Faith Clinic" each night, during which prayer cards would be distributed. This was before each evening's 7:30 p.m. "Mass Revival Rally," with its time of prayer for those needing healing.

During this particular crusade, Saturday night was designated "Holy Ghost Night," and a "Spiritual Gifts Service" would be held Sunday afternoon. Monday night was "Liberation Night," when Allen was scheduled to preach on "Can a Christian Be Demon-Possessed?" while "Stretcher Case Night" was scheduled for Wednesday evening. Allen made it clear that while individuals could seek for spiritual gifts during the "Spiritual Gifts Service," this should not be construed as suggesting that Allen had any connection with the Latter Rain Movement.

Allen did not characteristically mention other ministries or ministry movements by name from the pulpit, except for those directly associated with his ministry. He did make it clear, however, that he wished to have nothing to do with the Latter Rain Movement. "Not so-called 'latter rain,'" the ad emphatically declared.

The Latter Rain Movement was a revival movement the beginnings of which are generally traced back to events at the Sharon Orphanage and Schools in North Battleford, Saskatchewan in 1948. Recent historical studies have tended to lump together various strains of revivalism in the late '40s and early '50s, calling it all collectively "Latter Rain."

Those studies have attempted to link Billy Graham's early evangelistic endeavors, healing crusades by the likes of Oral Roberts, William Branham, and Jack Coe, Franklin Hall's emphasis on "Atomic Power" through fasting, and virtually any and every other revival movement of the period, despite their obviously disparate elements.

Modern researchers might even call A.A. Allen an adherent of the Latter Rain Movement. Clearly, however, Allen's 1955 ad made it clear that he, personally, believed otherwise.

The Latter Rain Movement can, however, be more narrowly defined. What Allen was probably referring to was a pronounced tendency for Latter Rain Movement leaders to focus on what has often been termed the "five-fold ministry," the idea being that those ministries are confirmed through the presence of prophecy and other spiritual gifts.

The "five-fold ministry" concept, which is still a popular theological notion today, is based on Ephesians 4:11. That passage, in the King James translation, reads "And he gave some, apostles; and some, prophets; and some, evangelists; and some, pastors and teachers."

As some would note, the strange punctuation in this passage was added by the King James translators and does not appear in the Greek text. A more direct translation, then, might read as follows: "And he gave some apostles, and some prophets, and some evangelists, and some pastors and teachers." The wording would seem to link pastors and teachers" together as a single ministry, thereby yielding a "four-fold ministry."

The fact that other scriptural passages refer to additional ministries does not seem to have diminished the popularity of the "five-fold ministry" concept, with some apparently eager to establish themselves as one of the "five-fold." First Corinthians 12:28 mentions that "God has set some in the church, first apostles, secondarily prophets, thirdly teachers, after that miracles, then gifts of healings, helps, governments, diversities of tongues."

Adherents of the Latter Rain Movement, however, tended to emphasize the role of the apostle and prophet, with some wishing to claim this "office," as termed in the King James translation, as supported by spiritual gifts. Further support would eventually be provided as we neared the end of the age, according to some Latter Rain theology, in the form of the "manifested sons of God." Allen clearly wished to distinguish the presence of the spiritual gifts, as practiced in his meetings, from those accompanying meetings of Latter Rain adherents.

A.A. Allen and the Assemblies of God butted heads at multiple points in his ministry career. In his stance against Latter Rain, however, he seems to have echoed Assemblies of God sentiments. The A/G's 23rd General Council, held in Seattle in 1949, passed a resolution specifically detailing points of contention regarding what that denomination called "The New Order of the Latter Rain" (in quotes).

The denomination pointed out that they were not opposed to visitations of God and times of revival. They took issue, however, with what they termed an "overemphasis" on "imparting, identifying, bestowing or confirming of gifts by the laying on of hands and prophecy." They also spoke out against what they saw as an "extreme and unscriptural" tendency toward "imparting or imposing personal leadings" through "gifts of utterance."[137]

Venturing into Television

Reports dated August 1955 from Allen's crusade in Durham, North Carolina told of an 11-year-old blind boy whose sight was restored, a polio victim removing her brace, the immediate disappearance of a huge tumor, and "wheel chairs emptied." Reports began to circulate to the effect that Allen had employed R.E. Kemery, "a top notch TV cameraman and technician," with the aim of starting television broadcasts. "Plans are now underway," it was announced, and "equipment is being purchased to record on sound film the miraculous which soon you will see on your TV sets."[138]

The year 1955 was a landmark year for A.A. Allen and his ministry organization. In 1955, the same year that he left the Voice of Healing organization, Allen's own magazine began. Known as *Miracle Magazine*, the first issue appeared in October of that year, and was subtitled "The Allen Revival News."

The magazine was not only used for promotion of his meetings, but *Miracle Magazine* also touted Allen's television series. Appearing in a red banner across the front of the first issue were the following words:

ANNOUNCING:

Miracles Today, the Allen Revival Telecast

Miracle Magazine, a new monthly publication[139]

The use of TV, in Allen's view, could help to fulfill the words of Matthew 24:14: "And this Gospel of the kingdom shall be preached in all the world for a witness unto all nations; and then shall the end come." In many of his television programs, Allen claimed that his programs featured recordings of the greatest miracles "ever recorded on sound film."

In his magazine, a photo appeared showing him in back of a pulpit mounded with reels of film, ready to be televised. That photo is captioned, "Here I am holding the first telecast, made in Fayetteville, N. C. On the pulpit are many more, ready to convince multitudes. Some of the greatest miracles ever witnessed are recorded on these sound films."[140]

Allen believed that God had given him a special mission regarding the use of TV. In fact, he declared that he had been given a supernatural message regarding his use of television:

> The miracle of TV is God's method to preach the gospel with signs and wonders to all nations. That is the thing which ultimately will bring to pass the greatest miracle of all, the return of Christ![141]

The inauguration of the Allen Revival Telecast occurred more or less simultaneously with the launch of *Miracle Magazine*. Allen's ministry organization had already published *Allen Revival News*, but his wife remarked in October of 1955 that they had only produced six issues of the earlier periodical during the previous two years.[142]

Steps were taken to prevent the public from assuming that Allen's separation from the Voice of Healing and his use of his own promotional apparatus in the form of TV broadcasts and a new magazine represented a rift in their views. *Voice of Healing* editor Gordon Lindsay issued a statement which appeared in the first issue of Allen's new magazine.

In part, Lindsay expressed good wishes to Allen in regard to his decision to go on TV. As Lindsay phrased it, "The editor of the *Voice of Healing* hereby expresses his sincere belief that your new step of faith will prove a great success."[143] Further, the first issue of Allen's new magazine featured a large and prominent promotion for the *Voice of Healing* magazine, with a subscription blank included.

Yet, in one sense it really was a rift. Controversial events in Knoxville, Tennessee, and the increasing realization that his ministry had grown too big to fit within the walls of a denominational structure — both literally and in terms of doctrine and practice — led to Allen creating his own support system and promotional network.

As Allen announced the launch of his TV series, his magazine listed the venture's key staff members. Among them was Robert Schambach, who would later become better known in his own TV and radio ministry as R.W. Schambach. Schambach, who had already worked with Allen in the latter's radio ministry, was made responsible for "Publicity and Advance Work" for the new television series.[144]

That job was shared with H. Kent Rogers, billed as "The World's Greatest Song Leader."[145] Jerry King acted as audio engineer and radio technician. This was Gerald W. King, Allen's brother in law, who later played a leading role at Miracle Valley, Allen's eventual ministry headquarters in Southern Arizona.

T. C. Anderson was introduced to the public as the original director of A.A. Allen's *Miracles Today* television series.[146] This was evangelist Tommy Anderson. In a number of Allen's TV programs, Anderson played piano, oftentimes alongside organist David Davis. Both men's music was featured later in various records produced onsite by the Miracle Valley record manufacturing plant.

A 1963 Allen camp meeting ad referred to Tommy C. Anderson as a "dynamic evangelist teaching each morning on operation of Holy Ghost and gifts of the Spirit!"[147] By the latter half of the 1960s, Anderson would be billed as "world Famous Evangelist Tommy Anderson" of Phoenix, Arizona.[148]

The television ministry of A.A. Allen would continue throughout the 1950s and 1960s. Evidently because of the criticism that was often directed against Allen, Allen continued to point to the presence of dramatic healings in his meetings as evidence that his ministry was of God.

His 1950s TV programs would include a feature that was present in his tent meetings: Allen would, on occasion, point to a banner overhead which quoted from the Bible: "No man can do these miracles except God be with him" (John 3:2). This statement also appeared in some of his newspaper ads. This same scripture hung on a banner overhead during Allen tent services even as late as 1969.[149]

The same basic idea was present in an undated flyer. That flyer was designed to promote Allen revival meetings in the Rock Island-Moline, Illinois area, while noting that Allen's ministry is

Being Confirmed by:

BIBLE MIRACLES (1 Cor. 12:28)

SIGNS AND WONDERS (Acts 5:12)

GIFTS OF HEALINGS (1 Cor. 12:28)

REVIVALS THAT STIR CITIES (Acts 8)[150]

Allen's approach, and this was exemplified by the contents of the same flyer, was to juxtapose healing testimonies and provocative sermon topics as a means of promotion.

"Those attending several nights in succession declare that all the 'spiritual gifts' are in operation," the flyer declared, "including miracles!" At the same, Allen was scheduled to speak on controversial subjects with titles like: "Blood to the Horses Bridles" "God's Last Message to a Fast Dying World," and "Has the World Already Passed God's Last Sign?"

Allen's message titled "Bargain Counter Religion," which was also released in book form, promised to be "a real revelation to all." In fact, it was to be "The night you have been waiting for:"

Is there more than one way to Heaven? Does Satan offer an "Easier," "Cheaper" way than Christ? Is it true that millions today have only "Bargain Counter Religion?" Know the truth![151]

Controversy in Knoxville

The year 1955 was not only a time for advances and successes in Allen's ministry. This was also a year of controversy over an event that is still commonly referred to as the "Knoxville Incident." During meetings in Knoxville, Tennessee late in the year,

Allen was arrested for drunk driving. Claims differ as to what actually happened, but some accounts raise serious questions to whether drunk driving actually occurred as charged.

The most commonly disseminated version seems to be that, while driving, Allen simply was pulled over by police for unstable driving. The police, according to standard accounts, found him to be drunk and placed him under arrest.

According to at least one writer, "Allen skipped bail rather than standing trial."[152] That same source goes further, to claim that Allen "tried to portray himself as victim of an elaborate kidnapping scheme."

No source is provided, however, for this latter assertion, and this conflicts with the account that Allen reportedly gave to ministry associate Paul J. Cunningham. News reports of the incident, as well as a closed file on the subject at the Flower Pentecostal Heritage Center (Assemblies of God Archives) do not appear to refer to any alleged "kidnapping scheme."

The press reported that Allen failed to appear in court on a drunk driving charge and, as a result, forfeited his $1,000 bond.[153] Cunningham, however, who worked closely with Allen in later years, said that he was told that Allen paid the fine uncontested rather than interrupt his meetings.[154]

Cunningham provided further information in a document he entered into the public record in Colorado Springs, Colorado:[155]

> Both Bro. Allen and H. Kent Rogers, (his vice president and crusade song leader) told me the same story, separate from each other.

> The Allen party was in revival in the Auditorium in Knoxville, Tenn. in the mid '50s. There was no church

large enough to accommodate the crowds, so the auditorium was chosen. The local pastors of the denomination he belonged to at that time, were clamoring for the "headquarters" to force Allen to come back into the churches, where he belonged. . . .

Bro. Allen drove from the motel in Knoxville, to the auditorium each night, accompanied by Bro. Rogers, and one or two others of the team. Since Allen did not eat before the service, he stopped at a local cafe on the way, to have a glass of milk.

This particular evening in question, he remarked to Rogers, "Rog, that milk tasted funny." Rogers responded, "perhaps it was blinky," meaning about to sour.

They then left the cafe for the meeting, and after driving a couple of blocks, Bro. Allen told Rogers, "I feel really dizzy, and think I'd better let someone else drive." He pulled over, and when he stopped, the media were there, accompanied by several denominational pastors, and the police (what a strange coincidence).

Cunningham's published remarks echo what he said in a personal interview. He said that Allen had been frequenting a particular cafe during the Knoxville meetings. One time while there, the milk tasted funny.

Allen then drove himself, which he rarely did, and started feeling dizzy. He pulled over as a result, and as he did so, according to Cunningham, he found himself surrounded by both police and Assemblies of God ministers. It became a matter of just paying a $245 fine on the one hand, or defending himself and interrupting his meetings on the other hand.[156]

According to Cunningham, Allen believed that he could not interrupt his meetings, which were already in progress, in order to stand trial. As a result, according to Cunningham's "public record,"

> Allen was then "ticketed" for DUI, and given a citation and allowed to proceed. He went to the auditorium, conducted the meetings, and in the following day's newspaper, the headlines screamed, "Evangelist Allen arrested for drunk driving."

Cunningham continued to explain that he was given this account by both A.A. Allen and by his Allen's ministry associate H. Kent Rogers:

> Allen and Rogers both told me this story, and that Allen simply "paid the ticket" and went on, rather than interrupt the schedule of meetings. They both felt that the goal of the "vendetta" was to "stop the Allen meetings." When the denomination demanded that Allen "stop his ministry," he refused, and "went independent." That meant an end to the large "tithe" they had been receiving, so they continued to attempt to "blackball" the Allen ministry.

Allen's ministry referred to the Knoxville matter as "unprecedented persecution."[157] His magazine claimed that a local newspaper, the *News Sentinel*, had conducted a "smear campaign" against Allen, but that the same paper had done something similar in 1946. Then, according to Allen's *Miracle Magazine*, the paper had attacked evangelist J. Harold Smith, labeling him a "racketeer preacher."[158]

Before the drunk driving charge was raised, according to Allen's magazine, Allen had been stopped by police over a traffic violation. Police, reporters, and photographers alike were said to have "converged" on Allen as he was driving, resulting in his being carried off to jail.

Because bail would not be accepted until 11 p.m., this meant he missed that evening's revival service. Allen was then, according to the magazine, subjected to "constant heckling" from reporters.[159]

During a later Knoxville meeting, according to Allen's *Miracle Magazine*, a hostile reporter began cursing outside the tent and was saved from "rough treatment" by "well-meaning friends" when one of Allen's "tent men" intervened.[160] This may have been the event that led to rumors that Allen's staff sometimes beat hostile reporters at his tent services.

Allen's ministry magazine claimed that during the trial over the drunk driving charge, the prosecuting attorney called and questioned a state's witness before the trial began and before witnesses had been sworn. This, according to the magazine, was while Allen's attorney was attempting to be granted a continuation in order to collect additional evidence.

The magazine claimed that the judge "sat back and smiled" while this occurred. Allen's magazine further charged that the bond was set at $250, five times the normal amount, and that a continuation would result in the bond being increased to $1,000.[161]

The story is told that rather than risk injuring the credibility of the Voice of Healing organization, Allen then withdrew from their membership and went independent. In fact, however, Allen created his own magazine before the Knoxville scandal. The same writer who claimed that Allen "tried to portray himself as victim of an elaborate kidnapping scheme" also claimed that afterward, Allen

> became increasingly paranoid, attacking his critics as atheists, communists, and unsympathetic to revivals. Stung by the criticism of other pentecostals, Allen even tried to set up a kind of denomination, Miracle Revival Fellowship . . . . [162]

This is, of course, just one interpretation, and it ignores the fact that Allen was already taking a hard-nosed, very public, and direct attitude against Communism before he ever arrived in Knoxville. In fact, this was clearly the case earlier in the same year of the so-called Knoxville Incident, in meetings in San Antonio. As already noted, in one of those earlier meetings Allen declared in an ad, "No Communists allowed on this night!" No one would be admitted unless they would "pledge they are not Communists!"

In addition, that interpretation ignores the fact that Allen was already, before the Knoxville meetings, speaking out against certain practices and beliefs of some other Pentecostals or Charismatics. That is why, as already noted, he said in one of his newspaper ads in 1955 before coming to Knoxville, that his "Spiritual Gifts Service" was "Not so-called latter rain."

Leaving the Assemblies of God was probably, for Allen, time for him to breathe a sigh of relief, despite his wife's insistence[163] that they remain within the denomination. Allen's ministry had grown too big for the Assemblies of God, and his increasing emphasis on "signs, wonders, miracles" did not seem to fit into the culture of the denomination.

Regarding the establishment of what the writer quoted above called "a kind of denomination," Allen's own Miracle Revival

Fellowship, sources seem to differ as to when this was established. When Allen died in 1970, the *New York Times* said[164] that Allen had "left the church" in 1954 for "his own - the Miracle Revival Fellowship." That date seems a bit too early, however, and denominational records of the Assemblies of God[165] show that he was credentialed by that denomination up until February 23, 1956.

Regardless of what actually happened in Knoxville, charges of alcoholism would continue to dog Allen and his ministry for the rest of his life. Paul J. Cunningham said that he had watched Allen's ministry closely, and that he could testify that it was a ministry of integrity.

Cunningham said that he never saw anyone keep a tighter schedule, and that this could not have been the case if Allen was an alcoholic. Allen worked hard, according to Cunningham. "He worked 20 hours every day," Cunningham said, and according to Cunningham, Allen believed that no one needed more than four hours sleep a night.

He added that he never saw anyone cast out more demons, and that he could not have done that if he was not of God.[166] It may be that Allen had criticisms like this in mind when he would, during his televised meetings, point to the large banner hanging overhead which quoted from John 3:2: " . . . no one can do these miracles . . . except God be with him."[167]

Unusual Manifestations

A unique feature of revival services associated with A.A. Allen was the appearance of oil on the hands of believers. This was a phenomenon which was touted as being a divine manifestation of God, and which was present, but only at times, by 1955.

The view of Paul Cunningham, who worked with Allen for a number of years, was that this was a genuine phenomenon from God. On the other hand, however, he cautioned that sometimes, among other groups, a counterfeit oil was manifested that was not of God.

When one church claimed that oil was being supernaturally manifested, but that it turned into a foul-smelling bloody mess when collected in containers, Cunningham told them that the oil was a counterfeit and admonished them to throw it out. Cunningham believed, however, that the oil present in Allen's services was the real thing.[168]

After five-year-old Lavin Burcham received the baptism of the Holy Spirit, he claimed that God was pouring oil onto his hands. Further, Allen claimed, if that oil could be applied to others and they would believe, they could be healed.[169]

According to Lavin's mother, traces of oil could be seen on the foreheads of those who had been prayed for by Lavin Burcham. Allen introduced Lavin to the crowds at his 1955 revival services in Greensboro, North Carolina, and in Los Angeles. Allen's magazine declared,

> . . . when the anointing of the Lord is heavily upon little Lavin, his hands leave traces of oil on the foreheads of those whom he touches. This is in itself a miracle. Although no oil is visible on his hands as he prays nevertheless at times as he touches the people there is oil on their foreheads.[170]

When Allen advertised tent meetings in Lynwood, in the Los Angeles area, in November of 1955, he emphasized the appearance of the "seven-year-old miracle boy" Lavin Burcham for the first time in the Los Angeles area. Burcham was touted as "the greatest modern miracle of our time."

> Hear his mother tell how God actually poured divinely created oil on the hands of this boy when he was only 5 years old and called him to heal the sick and perform miracles.[171]

Further, it was claimed, audiences at Allen's meetings in Los Angeles could expect a repeat of the sort of miraculous manifestations involving Burcham that were present a bit earlier in Knoxville, Tennessee: "This great miracle was repeated in the Allen revival in Knoxville last month. It will happen again in L.A."

Allen's ad asserted that a miracle will occur "when he touched you," as long as you have faith. This meant, however, that was absolutely necessary to get a special prayer card, in this case dubbed "miracle cards," in advance:

> You absolutely must get your "Miracle Cards" in advance to be ministered to on "Special Burcham Nights." Full info at tent only. No phone calls."[172]

Chapter 4:

A New Era Begins

In early 1956, Allen was still coming under fire from represen-tatives of established denominations as well as private citizens who felt threatened by Allen's highly public yet controversial methods. When he came to Phoenix, his detractors just as pub-licly demanded that he leave town after his January 24, 1956 healing service.[173] A group of local citizens cited four complaints:

(1) The revival has been keeping them awake until 11:30 at night.

(2) Cars carrying people to and from the revival are mak-ing too much dust.

(3) The traffic is a hazard to children.

(4) Unsanitary acts are being committed by persons attending the revival because of a lack of adequate lava-tory facilities.[174]

The city council was sympathetic to these requests, demanding that Allen leave right after the January 24th meeting. The council seemed to view this action as a compromise solution, since some were pushing for immediate revocation of the permit to erect the tent and to use temporary electrical connections.

In addition, Allen was told to end the meeting by 10, to make sure the PA system could not be heard off the lot, to reduce the dust raised by traffic, and to ensure that no additional "unsanitary acts" were committed. The city attorney pointed out, however, that these stipulations might be difficult to enforce, should Allen decide to defy them.

In addition, maximum fines that could be levied for any such infractions were only $300. Further, Allen's ministry team could have fired up a portable generator in the event that power would be cut off.[175]

The year 1956 was a landmark year for A.A. Allen's ministry. By this time, Allen had left the Assemblies of God churches for other and larger fields. As already mentioned, according to Paul Cunningham,[176] who worked with Allen in later years, Allen's meetings had outgrown all the Assemblies of God church buildings then in existence. Even the buildings used by the largest "A/G" congregations could no longer accommodate the crowds his meetings attracted.

Prominent "healing evangelist" Jack Coe died in 1956. When he died, Allen purchased Coe's tent, which seated about 18,000 to 20,000 persons.[177] This was likely the tent that Allen mentioned in his advertising in October of that year.

In prominent large letters, Allen announced that he was returning to Southern California "UNDER 200 x 300 FT. TENT," followed by the note that the tent was "Heated for your comfort."[178] At the same time, "all night" prayer meetings were to be held in the "big heated prayer tent."[179] This was presumably a separate tent, as appears to have been Allen's usual practice.

According to Paul J. Cunningham, who later worked with Allen at Allen's headquarters at Miracle Valley, the Assemblies of God (A/G) demanded that Allen return to their churches or they would pull his license. Allen told them that he could not return, simply because his meetings would no longer fit into their buildings.

According to Cunningham, the largest A/G auditorium at the time only sat 500.[180] In addition, the same ad that touted the 200 x 300-foot tent also made it clear that Allen's services were "Sponsored by the Largest Full Gospel Churches in the Los Angeles Area for All People of All Churches."[181] This was not a claim that could have been met had he restricted himself to Assemblies of God venues.

Ministerial credential files at the Flower Pentecostal Heritage Center at the Assemblies of God denominational headquarters in Springfield, Missouri[182] reveal that A.A. Allen was "no longer credentialed" as of February 23, 1956. The file also noted that he had been ordained by the denomination on February 13, 1942.

According to Cunningham, Allen's wife Lexie repeatedly urged him to return to the Assemblies of God. Cunningham said that Allen would patiently explain to his wife that he could not return: His meetings had grown too large to fit in any of the denomination's available facilities. He told her that he was not going back, that instead he was going on.

She was, however, in Cunningham's words, "married to the Assemblies of God." According to him, she could not accept his separation from the denomination. This appears to have only been the beginning of, ultimately, a rift between them. Eventually, according to Cunningham, Lexie tried to press her claim that Allen was insane, and tried three times to have him committed.

Cunningham said that the first time she had Allen brought into court, Allen's lawyer had Allen out of court within 15 minutes. Then she made two more attempts. Finally, his lawyer, according to Cunningham, suggested that she would eventually try this when the lawyer was unavailable, and that she would succeed before the lawyer could protect him.

Then, he suggested, according to Cunningham, that Allen would be put through shock therapy and that doctors would "fry" his brain. Allen then secured a divorce, according to Cunningham, and as a part of the settlement, Allen gave his wife their house and a substantial cash payment.

Allen, according to Cunningham, resisted the idea of divorce as long as he could, but finally chose that option in 1967.[183] Of course, this resulted in criticism that still echoes today. One comparatively recent writing,[184] for example, simply declares that in 1967 "he divorced his wife of more than thirty years," with no further explanation.

Actually, they separated in 1962, and later that same year sought a court decree of separate maintenance in Los Angeles. In addition, A.A. Allen's wife Lexie asked the court for $200 per week temporary alimony.

At the same time, Allen asked that Lexie be restrained from showing up at his services and from initiating proceedings to have him declared mentally unsound. Allen told the court that his wife had unsuccessfully tried this on two separate occasions in the past.[185]

Lexie told the court that her husband was worth over $150,000 — a considerable sum in those days — and that his income was $1200 per month. Allen, for his part, told the court that he had canceled a $250,000 life insurance policy made payable to A.A. Allen Revivals Corp. because of fear that he could be murdered for his money.

Some of the discussion in the court focused on money, with Lexie saying that much of what her husband owned came from what she termed "love offerings." Her husband said he would likely discontinue receiving them at his meetings, but was quoted as saying, "Love offerings depend on whether or not the people love you. If they love you, they will do something about it." He added that he could hardly stop someone from handing him a ten-dollar bill.[186]

Allen was ordered to pay his wife, the Rev. Lexie Allen, $600 a month in temporary alimony. The court also issued restraining orders against either party "annoying or molesting each other," as a newspaper put it, or "attending each other's services."[187]

Divorce was not something that Allen regarded as a viable option if it could, at all, be avoided. He had spoken out against divorce in one of his relatively early booklets, *Divorce: The Lying Demon*, subtitled *A New Approach to an Old Problem*. (The booklet is undated, but contains photos dated 1960.) In the booklet, Allen dealt with the subject of divorce as being inspired by demonic influence.

A comparison of Allen revival campaign promotions in 1956 with those just six years earlier shows a marked contrast. Earlier ads, from 1950, often emphasized the concept of a "'Back to

God' Revival and Healing Campaign" more than the person of A.A. Allen.

By early 1956, Allen was using a difference approach. A half-page ad[188] designed to promote Allen meetings in Fresno, California used "A.A. Allen" as the primary headline, followed by another heading that was nearly as large: "A National Revival."

"Signs - Wonders - Miracles" were also prominently proclaimed in this ad for the final week of meetings in the "big heated tent" at the Fresno County Fairgrounds. The formerly characteristic cut-out photo head shot of Allen was now replaced by a looming full figure of A.A. Allen over what appears to be a massive tent crowd. This was an image which would be repeated extensively throughout much of Allen's ministry.

A.A. Allen was drawing not only large crowds, but controversy as well. The year after the Knoxville incident, which appears to be still widely regarded as "proof" that Allen was an alcoholic, Allen was promoting dramatic healings through ads that tended to engender criticism.

"See this controversial figure on TV," one of his ministry ads[189] suggested early in 1956. This was for meetings in Fresno, where Allen would preach "an eye-opener sermon on 'The Religious Demon.'" From around this point in his career until the time of his death in 1970, Allen would become known for speaking out against what he saw as dead religion that he believed kept its adherents in bondage.

He remained strident and provocative: "Be present," the ad continued, "when Allen takes the lid off and exposes the reason why there are so many churches today that fight against one another." He also was scheduled to speak on "Will Russia Win the 'H' Bomb Race?"

Admittance by ticket ONLY! Tickets given away FREE to all who want to hear this Lecture. Stop at book stand for FREE tickets. No Communists allowed. Tickets given to Red Blooded Americans Only.

He would also be speaking on "My Vision of the Destruction of America." This message was based on a vision that Allen said he was given when he looked out across the vast expanse visible from the top of the Empire State Building. This vision centered around what he said would be an eventual military attack on the United States, and resulted in a book of the same title as the sermon.

During one night of the Fresno meetings, a "Holy Ghost Night" was planned. "Hundreds" would be "filled as Allen and Cooperating Preachers Lay Hands upon all those who desire to be filled."[190] Rev. B.E. Roberts, the pastor of the local Pentecostal Church of God, declared that "THIS MEETING IS PENTECOSTAL."

Another controversy erupted during the Fresno meetings, although it received only scant press coverage. A man claimed that he had been beaten with what a reporter described as a "deadly weapon" while visiting one of Allen's meetings. The "deadly weapon" turned out to be a flashlight.

Herbert Carlson, who was 51 years old, claimed that he was beaten by John M. McDonald, a 21-year-old ministry staff member, and that McDonald was assisted by two others. The accuracy of the claim and the incident's cause, if valid, was never made clear. McDonald said his shoulder was broken as a result of the alleged attack.[191]

Then when Pastor O. J. Phillips returned to his congregation in Compton, California, after attending the Fresno revival meetings, Phillips invited the public to attend his own services where similar supernatural manifestations were to be obtained. Phillips advertised his "Miracle Church," where meetings would be characterized by "God's Anointing Oil appearing on hands every service."

In addition, he noted, "SICK are being healed." He further informed potential visitors that his church was "cooperating" in the Oral Roberts healing campaign.[192]

Healing claims became even more provocative. When Allen appeared in April 1956 at the Miracle Church in Compton, California, a newspaper ad[193] pictured an ugly object that evidently was a tumor said to have left a woman's body. Because the object somewhat resembled a frog, the photo was captioned, "Miracle Church Presents...'The Miracle of the Unclean Spirit as a Frog Coming from Woman's Body."

Quoting from Allen's ministry publication *Miracle Magazine* in the ad, Allen asked the woman, "Are you sure this thing is a demon?" She replied,

> I don't know what it is but I do know it was on the inside of me. It moved around. It kicked. It scratched. It caused me much pain.

The woman, described as a "Christian woman from Utah," was to appear for a week in Allen's meetings in Compton.

A November 17, 1956 ad[194] for meetings in Buena Park, California, still used a heading Allen had employed before purchasing his tent: "Follow the Crowds." This was dwarfed, however, by a larger headline proclaiming simply "A.A. Allen." That was, in turn, followed by a much smaller tag line, "in person." Clearly he was widely known by this time and was in demand.

The caption "Under the World's Great Miracle Gospel Tent" follows the photo in that ad. Allen was described as "a man mightily anointed of God to bring deliverance to the sick." "Every night" was to be "a miracle night." This emphasis on healing would characterize his entire ministry.

At the same time, while earlier promotions might have referred the public to local radio broadcasts by local Assemblies of God pastors, now Allen had severed ties with the Assemblies of God. Now he was on his own, and the same 1956 ad was used to promote Allen's own TV and radio broadcasts.

The schedule for his daily meetings, held in a tent that was "comfortably heated," were outlined in the following terms: "Liberation and Fellowship" was scheduled for 10:30 in the morning, with ministry by various speakers on the subject of the spiritual gifts and their place in modern-day revivals. These meetings were led by the Rev. John E. Douglas.

Douglas is said to have become born-again through Allen's ministry.[195] After working with Allen's ministry for "several years," he then associated himself with the ministry of Juanita Coe, widow of well-known evangelist Jack Coe, who died in 1956. Evidently after Douglas's departure, his place was taken by Don Stewart, who would later play a prominent role in the Allen organizational leadership. [196]

Morning meetings were followed by afternoon meetings. This was when healing cards were distributed. The use of healing cards, sometimes called prayer cards, was a system in widespread use by various evangelists, and is a practice that persisted for decades. Kenneth E. Hagin was still employing this method in the 1990s.

In order to be prayed for to receive healing, each individual was required to have a prayer card. No one in these 1956 meetings was given a prayer card without having first attended the afternoon meeting. The purpose was to teach the word on healing and to prepare individuals to have faith to receive.

An undated Allen flyer advises "Those Seeking Healing or Deliverance in the Allen Meetings" to obtain a prayer card:

> Secure a card to enter prayer line at any instruction service. Allen reserves the right to pray at any time for people with outstanding faith. Those with little or no faith are encouraged to hold their cards until their faith has grown to a place of UNWAVERING STEADFASTNESS. These services build faith. Attend every one.[197]

Then, in the evening, came the "Miracle Revival Service." This was when "God's man of faith and power," as Allen was already known by this time, would minister. "Gifts of the Spirit," according to the 1956 ad, would be "operating in every service." Further, "Great miracles in evidence, thousands saved, healed, delivered. SIGNS, WONDERS, MIRACLES."

Another ad several days later[198] was similar, but this one emphasized a "special Miracles Week" featuring all-night prayer meetings. "Bring the HARD cases," the ad suggested, since "thousands" would be "praying for your deliverance."

This same promotion may have introduced wording that would be echoed repeatedly through verbal introductions by R.W. Schambach and other ministry associates just before Allen would take the platform.

The wording would be changed a bit from time to time, but the gist would stay the same: Allen was touted as the "man whom God raised up to spearhead a supernatural miracle revival." That revival move would, in later years, be invariably be referred to as a "miracle restoration revival."

Criticism Amidst Healings in the 1950s

Newspapers reported in 1956 that "strongarm attendants" of A.A. Allen had forced a *Sacramento Bee* reporter out of an Allen tent meeting. Evidently the photographers' efforts met with no objection as long as he was photographing healings, but once he began "taking pictures of money offerings," as one paper phrased it, he was removed from the meeting.[199]

Of course, photographing the collecting of an offering could involve significant privacy and security issues. The press, however, evidently saw this as evidence that Allen was trying to hide something, that being the amounts given in offerings. This incident is likely what formed the basis for later allegations that Allen routinely hired "goon squads" to "punch out" reporters. This claim found its way into the Wikipedia article on Allen prior to September 3, 2011.

In 1958, John H. Teeter, who called himself Executive Director of the Damon Runyon Memorial Fund for Cancer Research, wrote a letter which was published in a local paper in Eureka, California, the *Humboldt Standard*.

In the letter, Teeter had warned a certain Mrs. Walter C. Richcreek of Eureka against Allen. Her letter was evidently forwarded to the paper which then printed it. Teeter said that his organization had tried to assist "a Better Business Bureau," as he termed it, to gather information regarding a claim that a boy was able to see through a plastic eye as a result of Allen's ministry.

The letter also questioned a remark appearing in an issue of Allen's *Miracle Magazine*, claiming that a miracle of healing had been confirmed by a medical doctor of Hutchinson, Kansas. Teeter said that his organization was unable to find any record of this doctor by name, but the letter, as printed, spelled the name three different ways: Robert E. Alemore, Aelmore, and Achmore.

Teeter's view was clearly that A.A. Allen's ministry must be stopped. Regarding Allen, Teeter suggested that "Only the people of the local communities where he appears can stop these meetings."[200]

At some point during 1958, Allen rented a building from the Texas State Fair, where he held revival meetings. During those meetings, a number of individuals claimed healings, according to a later FBI report on Allen's activities.[201]

R.W. Schambach, who later became well known as an evangelist in his own right, worked with A.A. Allen for a number of years. Schambach frequently introduced Allen in tent crusades, as he often did on radio. On multiple occasions in later years, Schambach publicly reminisced about what he considered to be, as he put it, the greatest miracle he had ever personally witnessed.[202] This was a healing event that transpired during an Allen meeting in a fairgrounds auditorium in Birmingham, Alabama.

A mother brought her young son, age 4, who was said to be suffering from 26 major diseases. The child was born blind, deaf, and dumb, and he was born without feet and without male organs. His tongue hung out of his mouth. His lungs, liver, and heart were deformed, and only two and a half of his heart chambers were functional.

The child's arms and legs were deformed. His elbows protruded into his stomach as he would lay in a fetal position.

Schambach said that the baby had no reason to be alive. If the child was still alive at age four, Schambach reasoned, God must be planning to do a miracle. The woman brought the child to Allen's services, and stayed in a motel for a week. She attended all three services, every day and evening.

At one point, however, the woman came to Schambach and asked him, "Is the man going to pray for my son?" Schambach told her that he did not know. He knew that God tended to use Allen in supernatural ways during the services, but he could not know in advance what might occur.

The woman said she was down to her last $20. That included $15 for the doctor, and $5 for gas to get her home to Knoxville, Tennessee. Schambach told her he was unsure whether Allen would pray for the child in the meeting that night. If he did not, however, Schambach said he would personally take the child to the trailer where Allen was staying. Schambach noted, "We all lived in trailers."

That night, after R.W. Schambach introduced A.A. Allen, Allen said he believed that God was going to do great things. First, however, he wanted to, as Schambach put it, "give God an offering of faith." Schambach said he had never heard Allen use exactly that expression before. Allen explained that an offering of faith amounts to more than one can afford. If you can afford it, according to Allen, no faith is involved.

At that point, the woman handed her child to another woman and hurried forward to throw her offering into an offering bucket. Although she was sitting far back in the auditorium, she rushed forward to be the first one to give in the offering.

Schambach said that he was sufficiently nosy to look into the bucket. There he saw the woman's $20 - the last money she had. Schambach hurried behind the platform where, he said, he "wept like a baby," earnestly praying that he have the same faith that the woman had demonstrated.

After about ten minutes of preaching, Allen suddenly stopped. He explained that God was carrying him away in the Spirit. He said that he saw himself coming up to a white building which he recognized as a hospital. As he entered, he heard babies crying and realized that he was inside a maternity ward.

In the ward, a baby had just been born. About four or five doctors crowded around the baby. One of them said that the baby would not live beyond its first birthday. Then, Allen noted, the pronouncement was wrong, because the child was still alive.

Allen then saw a woman packing a suitcase and getting into an old Ford. The woman drove past the Tennessee-Alabama state line and eventually pulled into the parking lot at Allen's meeting. Allen then announced, as Schambach told the story, "Lady, you're here tonight. Bring me your baby now. God is going to give you 26 miracles."

Allen held the baby and asked everyone to close their eyes and pray. As Schambach told the story, he kept his eyes open, wanting to see what God was going to do. He recounted that the first thing he noticed was that the child's eyes seemed to contain what looked like tiny spinning whirlpools.

When the spinning stopped, Schambach saw perfect brown eyes. "If God opened the eyes," Schambach reasoned, "I knew them deaf ears popped." Then Schambach noticed a cracking sound. The arms moved out into normal position. So did the legs. Feet appeared where there were no feet.

In a similar fashion, a woman who had a breast medically removed came for prayer, asking that it be restored. As televised, of course the woman was fully clothed, but was obviously emotionally overcome. Her testimony was that the breast did indeed grow back.[203] Paul Cunningham, who worked with Allen at the time, said in later years that the healing was affirmed at the time to have been genuine.[204]

Allen didn't just ask audiences to believe for physical healing. He admonished congregations to believe for deliverance from any "mountain," as mentioned in Mark 11:23:

> For truly I say to you, that whoever will say to this mountain be removed and be cast into the sea, and will not doubt in his heart but will believe that those things which he says will come to pass, he will have whatever he says."

As Allen expressed it, a mountain could be sickness.

It could be disease. It could be infirmity. A mountain could be a backslidden husband or a rebellious wife. It could be children that refuse to follow in the footsteps of mother and daddy. A mountain could be a financial problem. A mountain could be a broken heart, a depressed spirit, that causes you to be depressed, restless, sleeplessness, aimless wandering.[205]

Allen believed that the Bible promised freedom from any such "mountains."

Chapter 5:

The Birth
of Miracle Valley

About the last decade and a half of Allen's life were characterized by being the leading figure in a faith community of believers. That community was known as Miracle Valley, which served as not only Allen's ministry headquarters, but home to numerous individuals and families of similar beliefs. Miracle Valley was also home to a Bible college started by Allen.

In a very real way, then, Miracle Valley began to take on a life of its own, and to extend the ministry of A.A. Allen in ways far beyond what could be accomplished by any one man. Paul Cunningham, who worked with Allen, explained that it was because of extensive prayer involving large numbers of individuals at Miracle Valley during camp meetings that dramatic healings took place. It was not just a matter of Allen's ministry, but rather a matter of collective prayer which, in some cases, went on all night long.

The land where Miracle Valley would be situated is located in Cochise County, Arizona, about 15 miles west of the small town of Bisbee. Urbane Leiendecker, a rancher who appreciated Allen's ministry, donated the first 1200 acres of what would become 2400 acres set aside for Miracle Valley. The remaining 1200 acres were bought by Allen from Leiendecker's brother Ben, for an amount reported to be $45,000.[206]

Allen later recalled, "And in 19 and 58 it was the desire of my heart to have a huge piece of property or a piece of land whereby we could build a great Bible training center and house A.A. Allen Revivals, Inc."[207] An undated promotional film titled *This is Miracle Valley* later emphasized the role of the site in housing Allen's Bible College:

> This growing community is a living monument to the faith and dedication of the anointed ministry of Evangelist A.A. Allen. From all sections of the United States and from many foreign lands, hundreds of dedicated young men and young women have come to study in these classrooms, to worship together in the college chapel, and to prepare themselves for a miracle ministry to the nations.[208]

David Hollis, who had worked for Allen in Dallas, was at Allen's new ministry location at Miracle Valley when use of the site began. He recalls that the earliest buildings were all mobile homes.[209] A bit later, cinder blocks for new construction were produced on the site.

The Growth of Miracle Valley

Despite the rise of anti-Allen controversy by the late '50s, his ministry headquarters, Miracle Valley, continued to grow. In an article copied more or less verbatim but under various similar titles in various newspapers, Miracle Valley was established in the summer of 1958 as "a 'City of God.'"[210]

The same papers noted that "frivolities" such as "liquor, lipstick, tobacco and ornate jewelry" were forbidden in this unique community. More than a decade later, in 1969, *Time* magazine would refer to Miracle Valley as a "teetotaling, nonsmoking oasis of evangelistic fervor and hard-nosed business."[211]

Allen held tent revival meetings in January of the next year, 1959, in Phoenix. This series of meetings may have been designed to give local citizens first-hand familiarity with the Allen ministry in an attempt to boost Miracle Valley's relationship with the local community. That seems especially likely considering that promotions for the Phoenix meetings were tied to a special "Miracle Week" to be held later that month at Miracle Valley.[212]

Another reason why a public relations aim may have been part of the reason behind the Phoenix meetings is that advertising made a special appeal to area churches and ministers:

> This great meeting is set apart for all ministers of all denominations from all parts of the world. To gather together to fast and pray for the purpose of seeing revival in our time! MINISTERS and people of all churches in Phoenix area cordially invited.

This was while it was being announced that immediately following (beginning the day after the Phoenix services ended), the Miracle Valley "Miracle Week" would commence. Further, reservations could "now" be made:

SPECIAL! BEGINNING Jan. 19th Thru Jan. 25th

At MIRCLE VALLEY FOR ONE WEEK ONLY

Location: Between Bisbee and Fry (now called Sierra Vista) on Highway 92. Rooms and Meals will be available on the Grounds. Make reservations now at the tent. Come to Miracle Valley. A Miracle Week.

In addition, it was made clear that the Allen meetings in Phoenix were being held in cooperation with local "full gospel" churches:

FOR ALL PEOPLE OF ALL CHURCHES

Sponsored By Full Gospel Churches of Phoenix Area[213]

Allen held similar meetings a few months later (March 31 through April 2, 1959) in Winnipeg, Manitoba, far from the turmoil and controversy which surrounded the establishment of Miracle Valley. He then placed a similar newspaper display ad, but it made no mention of support from local pastors. No appeal was offered to local ministers, specifically, to join in prayer for revival.

In the same month as the Phoenix meetings, January of 1959, A.A. Allen's son James was said to be acting as Miracle Valley's administrator. He was quoted as saying that the numbers who had made the move to Miracle Valley would be even higher if it were not for the fact that some applicants did not possess the "religious fervor and sincerity of motive" that Allen's ministry desired.[214]

By this time, Miracle Valley was boasting a population of about 300, up from half that figure in October of the previous year. Not only that, but it was reported that "newcomers are arriving weekly."

More than a fourth of the residents were said to be students of Miracle Valley's Bible school. Miracle Valley was then occupying about 2400 acres. Half of the land was donated by Urbane (also known as Urban) Leiendecker. The rest was said to have been purchased by Allen from Urbane's brother Ben for a reported $45,000.[215]

Included in the land from Urbane Leiendecker was a ranch house which papers reported was now being used for "light industry." That included a mattress factory and a phonograph record manufacturing plant.[216] This appears to have been the same ranch house which, in the 2010s, was occupied by Miracle Valley Arizona Ministries, headed by Gilles and Diane Langevin, along with their son Michael, while seeking the funds needed to restore the property.[217]

By January of 1959, Miracle Valley residents were said to be making their own cinder blocks for construction purposes. In addition, "a few irrigated crops" were already being grown, and about 100 head of cattle were grazing on Miracle Valley's range.

A grammar school and a high school were already in use. The high school's dean of women was Ada Tyssowski, daughter of missionaries to Hawaii. Construction at Miracle Valley was described in terms of a growing "town:"

> Last fall the budding religious settlement had three or four new cinder block buildings and a score or so of house trailers. Today there are seven permanent buildings, another under construction and about 50 trailers.

A church also is being built. Stores, factories, and a town hall are planned.[218]

In early May of 1959, the number of residents at Miracle Valley were reported to be around 300, up from 150 the previous October.[219] Of those 300, more than a fourth were students of Miracle Valley's Bible school. By August of that year, Allen was making plans to move his ministry headquarters from Dallas to Miracle Valley.[220]

As mentioned earlier, A.A. Allen pitched his tent for special meetings in Winnipeg, Manitoba in March, for meetings from March 31st through April 2nd. There held held three services daily, with a "Liberation Service" scheduled at 10:30 each morning, a "Faith Clinic" at 2:30 pm (when prayer cards would be distributed), and a spectacular "Miracle Rally" each evening at 7:30. "Every night a miracle night," an ad proclaimed.[221]

Those meetings ended April 2nd, then it was on to Greensboro, North Carolina, where Allen again held meetings. This time, however, the location was not the Allen tent, but the Guilford Tobacco Warehouse. Allen followed exactly the same schedule as he had employed in Winnipeg for these meetings scheduled for April 15-26.[222] The announcement was made that "Miracles Take Place Instantly as Allen Prays the Prayer of Faith."[223]

Tension with the Local Community

Attempts by Miracle Valley's staff to heighten relationships with the outside community continued through 1959. "Cards of Thanks" to merchants who "made contributions to our organization" were placed in newspapers in May by Leila B. Wallace, "Missionary," signing "on behalf of the Miracle Valley Bible Training Center."[224]

Tension with the local community erupted later that year, however, when residents of the neighborhood around Miracle Valley became concerned about what a Phoenix paper called "amplified revivals."[225] That same source reported that the county attorney was led by "numerous petitioners" to file a disturbance of the peace complaint against Urbane Leiendecker, the man who had donated the land for Miracle Valley to A.A. Allen.

Why the complaint was directed against Leiendecker rather than Allen is not clear. The "noise" from revival meetings, according to testimony, could be heard for two miles. The witness claimed that the sound was "almost deafening a quarter-mile away." He added that, "The noise wakes the youngsters at night and disturbs the neighbors."

Although some neighbors claimed that the revival meetings could be heard at all hours of the night, Leiendecker was cited as saying that no preaching continued past 10 p.m. He added, "I make no apology for preaching the gospel of Jesus Christ."

In other respects, the relationship between Miracle Valley and the surrounding community appears to have been less troublesome. A high school was operated at the site, which advertised its graduation ceremonies in the local paper. The undated film *This is Miracle Valley*, produced by Allen's organization, portrays life at Allen's ministry headquarters as one characterized by tranquility and industry.

Mornings typically began with a time referred to by Gerald W. King, Allen's executive director, as "our morning devotion:"

This is the time of the day we set apart that we consider the most important time of our work here at Miracle Valley, and that is our morning devotion. . . . We consider this the most important few minutes that we spend before God. Not only that, at this time we join with Brother Allen in praying for the many prayer requests that come from across the country and across the nation, in meeting the needs of the multitude of people.[226]

The staff would then pray over the many prayer requests that had been mailed to Miracle Valley.

The documentary film *This is Miracle Valley* provides an overview of the offices and business organization of Allen's ministry at the time:

> The business offices of the Allen Revival organization were moved to Miracle Valley, Arizona to provide part-time employment for many Bible College students. These students work under the guidance of Evelyn Kampfer, the personnel manager.

Much of the work of Allen's organization appears to have centered around the mailing of his magazine, *Miracle Magazine*, as well as tracts, books, and record albums:

> The name of each subscriber to *Miracle Magazine* is entered on its own individual addressing stencil. Careful records are kept to make certain that each subscriber receives every issue of *Miracle Magazine*.

> Many thousands of record albums are produced and sent out from Miracle Valley to the growing number of radio listeners and television viewers who desire to have the anointed, inspiring music of these miracle revivals continually in their homes.

> More millions are learning to read every year, and Rev. Allen sends many thousands of books and hundreds of

thousands of tracts to spread the word of God throughout the entire world.

The "modern printing plant" at Miracle Valley was said to "provide employment for a number of students from the Bible College." Other departments included the Art Department, charged with designing book covers, and the Publications and Typesetting Departments.

In addition, reel-to-reel tapes of A.A. Allen's radio broadcasts were shipped out to radio stations from Miracle Valley:

> The *Allen Revival Hour* is heard on many radio stations, heard by millions of listeners around the world. Students are trained to operate these high speed tape duplicating machines which reproduce the radio broadcasts.

Television films of past broadcasts were also "filed for future use." These were "made available to missionaries and evangelists" who used them as ministry tools.[227]

Record albums of music and preaching from Miracle Valley were produced on-site. Those records today, when they can be found, appear to be popular with collectors. Part of that seems to be because of the high demand for Allen materials as well as materials pertaining to other ministries of "faith and power." Another reason for the record albums' popularity with collectors stems from Miracle Valley's tendency to use what *This is Miracle Valley* terms "the highest quality vinyl" in bright, sometimes translucent, colors:

> Miracle Valley has its own recording company and record factory, producing many thousands of Christian record albums. A worker places first the labels, and then a biscuit of highest quality vinyl on the stamping machine.

Heat and pressure are applied from a steam boiler and, lo, a miracle occurs. The biscuit of vinyl is changed into a beautiful record. It is then slipped into its protective jacket and sealed until the moment when, at final delivery, another inspirational record from Miracle Valley will bless another Christian home.

The records are packed into boxes and stored in the warehouse, ready for shipment to any part of the nation or the world. And remember, better Christian music will make better Christian homes, and better Christian homes will make a better world.

Over a decade after Allen and his team first arrived at Miracle Valley, *Time* magazine described the business aspects of the Allen operation in terms that were remarkably similar to those presented in the film *This is Miracle Valley*. A 1969 article in *Time* magazine noted 100 students enrolled in the Bible college at Miracle Valley, "squads" of secretaries, clerks, and printers in the busy ministry headquarters, and "banks" of file card drawers, automatic typewriters, and printing presses.[228]

That article claimed that the organization was mailing over 55 million pieces of literature a year. Allen's programs were said at the time to be on 43 TV stations and 53 radio stations.

The record plant at Miracle Valley was making 47 titles available, a Cessna 150 was at the ministry's own airstrip, and 17-day camp meetings were being held twice annually in the 3,000-capacity tabernacle.

In roughly similar terms, *Look* magazine the same year (1969) noted that the "Information Booth" just inside Allen's tent offered 47 record albums and 50 or so books. At Miracle Valley, according to the same source, 175 employees were responsible for those LPs and books, as well as radio and TV programs and other media materials. The staff also managed Allen's correspondence course program, with around 15,000 students.[229]

Allen was still holding tent revivals in 1959, and was still using the Bible slogan, taken from John 3:2, "No man can do these miracles except God be with him." He was still being referred to in advertising as "God's man of faith and power." His tent, at the time, was still being touted as "one of the world's largest tents."[230] Ads the following year, in 1960, boldly claimed that he was using the "world's largest tent."[231]

Even a decade later, in 1969, a fleet of five moving vans labeled "A.A. Allen Revivals" were being used to transport a huge tent and other ministry materials, as well as equipment, to remote locations. A 1969 article in *Time* magazine noted Allen's use of "advance men,"[232] but this has been a common job title associated with evangelistic campaigns going back into the 19th century.

Additional Noteworthy Healings

Countless claims to healing were associated with the Allen ministry over the years, some much more prominent than others. Of many that could be cited, two that immediately leap to mind are those of Gene Mullenax in the 1970s and, much earlier, Leroy Jenkins in 1960.

Surgeons had removed the right lung and three ribs from Mullenax. A large hole, said to be big enough that a man's hand could fit inside, had been left in his back for a drainage tube. Doctors did not think he had long to live.

Mullenax was still able to drive, however, and at one point in May 1958 he passed what he thought was a circus tent set up in Little Rock. He entered the tent and found himself in the middle of an A.A. Allen tent revival meeting. While there, he witnessed what appeared to be a number of dramatic healings.

He returned to the tent for several days, his wife accompanying him because he had grown too weak to attend alone. He was skeptical, yet kept attending. Finally, he obtained a prayer card and entered the healing line, while still plagued by doubts. He was determined to speak out against Allen, grabbing his microphone and declaring that Allen was a fake, if nothing happened.

While waiting in line, Gene Mullenax saw a large tumor instantly disappear from the face of a baby who had been in the line immediately in front of him. Then it was Gene's turn. Despite his doubts, Mullenax found himself raising his arms and sobbing. As he did so, it felt like a thick oil had been poured over him. Suddenly he was healed.

When his 185-pound best friend joined him on the stage, Mullenax picked him up. Up to this point he had been unable to even hold his 6-month-old baby without hemorrhaging. Mullenax claimed that missing body parts simply "went back in."[233]

Nancy Mullenax, Gene's wife, said in later years that before her husband had this experience, they did not believe in "anything like that."[234] The incident had upended their theology. Gene Mullenax eventually entered ministry.

Four years after the incident, Allen's *Miracle Magazine* published the news that Gene Mullenax had kept his healing. A doctor was quoting as saying that x-rays showed that the missing lung and ribs had indeed been replaced.[235] In the early 21st century he was still healed.

Jenkins was working on his house in Atlanta on Mother's Day in 1960 when a sheet of window glass broke and fell. The glass cut through flesh and bone in the area of Leroy Jenkins' right arm, severing arteries.

After he was rushed to a hospital, Jenkins believed he had "a near-death experience" in which he left his body and saw the doctors attempting to restore him to health. Those doctors were able to reattach his arm and to send him home, but informed him that he would soon die of gangrene poisoning, since his arteries were severed.

At the time, A.A. Allen was conducting revival meetings at the Atlanta Fairgrounds in a tent that held about 8,000 people. Leroy Jenkins was taken there "in agony, with his arm putrefying within the cast."[236]

After Jenkins was told by Allen, "Young man, tell these people that God will heal you," the nervous and apprehensive Jenkins managed to get out the words, "God's going to heal my hand."

At that moment, according to Jenkins' testimony,[237] "the tent appeared to split open, and a giant hand appeared." Jenkins believed that if that hand would touch him, he would be healed. His lifeless fingers then began to move.

Allen responded with, "Look at him. He's using that dead hand. God has healed him and I didn't even pray for him!" Jenkins then touched a woman with a broken wrist, and she was instantly healed. This, according to Jenkins, was the beginning of what became his own healing ministry. Jenkins became known as "the man with the miracle arm."

When Jenkins held a crusade in El Paso twelve years later, newspaper ads claimed that his meetings constituted the "Greatest Evangelistic Crusade in History" involving "the world's most unusual ministry."[238]

Ads invited the crowds to "Witness miraculous healings! Hear inspiring testimonies! Every service is a miracle service!" Jenkins' ministry was touted as being "an exciting phenomenon of the 20th Century" as he was "blessed with the divine gifts of healing and knowledge."

By the 21st century, the ministry of Leroy Jenkins was being called into question by some. Prominent in controversy was his use of "miracle water:" small bottles of water which Jenkins promoted as a means of receiving healing.

Miracle water was being sold by the bottle or by the case. One woman attending one of his meetings wondered aloud, however, why she would need a whole case if it really is "miracle" water. A controversy with the Ohio Department of Agriculture in 2003 centered around whether the water was safe for drinking.[239]

The life of Leroy Jenkins became the subject of a feature-length motion picture in 2002 with the release of *The Calling*, released on DVD as *Man of Faith*. This two-hour (1 hour and 59 minutes) film was directed by Damian Chapa, who also plays the part of Leroy Jenkins in the film.

In addition to Leroy Jenkins, another individual of note first became associated with Allen's ministry in 1960,[240] and that was Curtis Eugene Martin, known as Gene Martin. Allen explained how Martin came to enter a prominent music ministry with Allen's organization: "I found him in a tent meeting in Atlanta several years ago. Above the thousands of voices singing in that tent, one soared above all the others." He said that it took a while to find out who was responsible, but "From the moment we located Brother Martin, he became a member of our team."[241]

As an African-American, Martin himself countered claims that he was in a racially oppressive position by working for a white man, A.A. Allen. "Some folks say I'm just a monkey on a string," Martin noted. "I'm not a monkey, but even if I were, I'd still be a whole lot better off than those hypocritical church members and backsliders, because I'd be Jesus' monkey."[242]

By 1961, Allen claimed that he was using the "world's largest tent" and that he was accompanied by "the world's greatest miracle revival evangelistic party."[243] Promotions publicizing his Tucson meetings in February of that year announced that "SIGNS WONDERS MIRACLES according to the Bible" could be expected. Even at this late day, Allen was still quoting John 3:2 in his advertising: "No man can do these miracles except God be with him."

That quote accompanied Allen, at least off and on, in his ministry for many years. It appeared over the heads of his audience in his tent campaigns. He quoted it on TV. Perhaps Allen was attempting to address the skepticism that he knew persisted in the minds of many of his congregations, the same skepticism back when he first attended an Oral Roberts tent campaign.

Perhaps he was also attempting to make sure his audiences realized that he was not trying to claim any personal power to heal. As his ministry associate Ross Collette phrased it in 1970,

Brother Allen sort of expects people to be skeptical. We're not trying to prove anything to the skeptics. We don't take any elaborate pains to prove anything to anybody. Brother Allen doesn't claim to be a healer. He always says he couldn't heal a fly with a headache. He's not claiming to be another Jesus Christ, because he's not. It's God that cures the sick.[244]

Once Miracle Valley was extensively developed, meetings were held there, in the community's "tabernacle." That facility, which still stands, not only housed a large auditorium, but a stairway in the entry foyer led to a second story "prayer tower."

Other meetings were still held in various other cities, however. As a typical example, the 1961 Tucson revival, for instance, featured an intensive calendar of special meetings: "Holy Ghost Night," "Youth Renew Night," "Mass Miracle Night," "Liberation Night," and "Double Portion Night." A "Special Miracles Night" was also included, as well as a "Spiritual Girts Receiving Service" and "Proxy Night," explained as "when you come for another."

For those who were in particularly desperate circumstances and in need of healing or deliverance, "private interviews with A.A. Allen" were offered in the afternoon service. This was when "prayer cards" were given for those who wished to be admitted to the healing line in the evening service.

These meetings were held in a Tucson facility, the Temple of Music and Arts. This was to be followed, however, by a "Miracle Week" at nearby Miracle Valley.[245]

As another example, Allen meetings in 1962 were held in Toronto in the Palace Pier, described by a Canadian newspaper as being "usually a gay centre of dancing and partying." The paper noted that, with "as many as 1,000 attending a single session," claims of healing had been a part of the Toronto meetings. The paper, obviously skeptical, said that "Several persons have been 'treated' by the 'laying on of hands' common in faith healing circles."[246]

It seems to have been at Miracle Valley, however, that Allen felt particularly free to finally pursue his own views. One factor that continually characterized Allen's ministry in general, however, was the fact that he was unafraid to critically confront organized traditional religion.

Allen and "Miracle Restoration Revival"

He and his associate Clarence Mitchell had come out against what Mitchell termed "Starving Sheep and Overfed Shepherds," the title of a Mitchell book published by Allen. Allen continued to take an unrelenting stance against what he viewed as dead religion, boldly declaring that some of the most vocal opponents of revival are religious people:

> Remember, enemies of the Gospel (sometimes disguised as religious people) are at work to bring powerful forces against Christians and Preachers who stand for Healing and Miracles!

In keeping with Cold War philosophy, such negative forces were tied to socialistic forces:

> Don't forget, our constitutional rights of religious freedom are being severely challenged by forces that want a government controlled church in America![247]

One constant theme in Allen's theology that in particular invited criticism was his unrelenting criticism of denominationalism and what he saw as dead religion. In 1963, his ministry organization at Miracle Valley published Clarence G. Mitchell's book which epitomized this view.

The same year, Allen published a closely related book which he had penned, titled *Prisons with Stained Glass Windows*. Allen's unrelenting criticism of denominationalism and of "dead religion," which he saw as going hand-in-hand, was a recurring theme in his ministry. Of course, it fueled much of the widespread criticism that was directed against him and against Miracle Valley by some representing established denominational religion.

This theme was discussed by Allen in his 1967 book *Bargain Counter Religion*. Even more to the point was an undated booklet by Allen, titled *Let My People Go!* The booklet's cover includes a synopsis of its contents:

Tradition or restoration revival - which?

Exposes the sin of denominational tradition today.

Proves that revival will never come to the church denominations bound by the tradition of the elders

Answers the question, "Why do denominational preachers fight miracle revival?"

Will give the reason preachers stick to their man-made organizations and will never be free

What does God say about real Pentecostal manifestations?[248]

Although *Let My People Go!* is undated, Allen refers to what he calls the "latest Move of God," which he said had begun in 1969 at Miracle Valley. This "move" was what he referred to as the "Let My People Go! campaign."

"Let my people go! Loose them from your doctrinal bondages, your financial burdens, your false doctrines, your constitutions and by-laws, as well as your papal encyclicals, your denominational authority, which engender all their fears." With this dramatic demand I launched an intensive campaign against the grip of denominational bondage which has hampered the people of God for these past hundreds of years.[249]

The message of *Let My People Go!* was further amplified by Mitchell's book, which was published and distributed by A.A. Allen Revivals, Inc. The book, dated 1963, was given the provocative title of *Starving Sheep and Overfed Shepherds*, and was promoted on Allen's television programs. Mitchell was also author of a similar undated treatise titled *The Battle for Supernatural Ministry and Worship in Our Day.*

Rev. Clarence G. Michell was born in 1919 and died in 1982, according to his tombstone at Greenwood Memorial Park in Ft. Worth, Texas.[250] Mitchell was himself an evangelist.

Although Mitchell's anti-denominational leanings may have come a bit later, a newspaper display ad dating from as early as 1956 promotes the second week of revival meetings featuring Clarence G. Mitchell at First Assembly of God in Big Spring, Texas.[251] The previous year, Mitchell had led a revival at the Frisco Assembly of God in Frisco, Texas.[252]

The criticism of "overfed shepherds" was an integral part of the concept which Allen had been promoting at least as early as the 1950s as what he termed "restoration revival." The idea behind the term was that relatively dead churches had neglected the supernatural power of God, but that this power was now being restored.

Paul J. Cunningham, who appeared on the platform with Allen in a number of meetings at Miracle Valley, said later that he and others at Miracle Valley believed that they had entered a revival - a "miracle restoration revival" - which would culminate in the return of the Lord.[253] At the heart of that revival movement was the full restoration of every sort of miracle discussed in the Bible.

The essential concept of what Allen called "restoration revival" was outlined as early as August 1954 in the pages of *The Voice of Healing* magazine, although Allen at that time simply referred to it as "revival." He saw this as a pivotal historical event which would bring the church into a new epoch:

> God has [been] and is raising up men with a positive message that are being used of God to bring about a REVIVAL that is the greatest in the history of the church.

This was contrasted with those in the body of Christ who were not sympathetic to the tenets of "restoration revival:"

> Of course, there are a few here and there who are so bound by coldness, indifference, skepticism, modernism, and by the boundaries of sectarianism that they have failed to see, or else are unwilling to confess, that God is on the move and multitudes are moving with Him!

In discussing this, Allen kept an eye on persecution of his own ministry, a factor which only seemed to accelerate throughout the years of his ministry:

> But while some oppose this mighty moving of God's spirit, and even some leaders openly declare that it is not of God nor from heaven, God continues to pour out his Spirit on ALL FLESH! While some declare, "I don't believe in this ministry of deliverance," is busy delivering the multitudes . . . . [254]

Additional Attacks on Allen

Criticism continued against the healings present in Allen's meetings continued. When 22-year-old Carl Johnson died at

Miracle Valley in 1963 after attempting to obtain divine healing, this was seen as evidence that Allen's views were dangerous. Johnson was described as a "student"[255] of Allen, but whether this meant that he was attending Allen's Bible College at Miracle Valley at the time is not clear.

Johnson had been advised by a local doctor to submit to hospitalization, but Johnson was unable to afford to do so and had no insurance. A news story headed "Liver Ailment Fatal to Student of Faith Healer" seemed to cast broad aspersions against Allen, but without saying how Allen could have been personally to blame.

Around the same time, the Allen ministry organization was hit with an Internal Revenue Service claim that the organization owed $380,000 in income tax. The government claimed that A.A. Allen Revivals, Inc. was established to benefit Allen, his wife, and "their associates."[256] Allen, on the other hand, claimed that his ministry organization deserved tax-exempt status.

Not only was Allen's ministry directly attacked by criticism, but indirectly, whenever his followers engaged in excess or unfounded fanaticism. An Ohio couple, for example, made the local papers[257] after they believed that a clerical error which indicated that their car was paid for was a miracle from God.

The couple, Mr. and Mrs. William C. Graessle, said that they had been vacationing at Miracle Valley when Mr. Graessle was told that he would receive a miracle if he made a sacrifice. Graessle left an offering of $5 and expected a miracle.

The Lima, Ohio office of General Motors Acceptance Corporation (GMAC) kept its file on the Graessle car loan next to records on a certain Clarence F. Whetstone. When Whetstone made a payment, his payment was mistakenly recorded in

Graessle's record. When the Graessles received a check in the mail for overpayment to GMAC, along with the canceled mortgage and clear title to their car, they assumed that this was their miracle.

A considerable time later, GMAC caught the error and tried to convince the couple that they still owed 23 payments of $75.91. Meanwhile, GMAC obtained an injunction restraining the Graessles from selling the car. This was at the same time that an equity suit was filed against them.

While the court decided that the couple did indeed have to make the remaining payments, the rebate check for $167.79 was overlooked. Evidently, at least as suggested by one newspaper account, the couple was able to cash the check. Assuming that this was the case, then although the couple was more-or-less ridiculed by the press, it would appear that their $5 investment did yield a $167.79 return.

Criticism against A.A. Allen revival meetings were, by 1963, being reflected in his advertising. A full-page display ad for services held in Baltimore July 26 through August 25, 1963, promoted as "FOUR FULL WEEKS of Summer Campmeeting," advised the public to ignore "poison pen" comments against Allen and his ministry:

DON'T BE DECEIVED BY PROPAGANDA!

DON'T BE MISLED BY "POISON PEN" WRITERS!

DON'T LET RUSSIA BRAINWASH YOU IN A CHURCH WASH PAN!

Remember, enemies of the Gospel (sometimes disguised as religious people) are at work to bring powerful forces against Christians and Preachers who stand for Healing and Miracles! . . .

The ad further suggested that media criticism directed against Allen could represent a part of a Communist conspiracy:

Here are partial quotes from *Brainwashing*[,] a book with part of Russia's instructions for destroying the Church in America! "Ridicule and Defame the Preachers if they Advertise a Healing Campaign call it a hoax; the Church, especially the Healing Campaign, must be destroyed, even if you have to resort to wild lies, personal defamations, false evidences, and constant (bad) propaganda!"

Readers were then pointedly asked, "HAVE YOU BEEN BRAINWASHED BY THESE METHODS?"[258] Allen was sticking to his guns despite the unique two-way flow of communication that characterized his ministry by this time: Allen was unrelenting in his attacks against denominationalism and what he considered to be dead churches, while the church world continued to criticize Allen. Still, Allen continued to point to the same scripture he had been quoting since the '50s: "No man can do these miracles except God be with him." (John 3:2).[259]

Throughout at least most of his ministry career, the healing ministry of A.A. Allen drew criticism. A Church of Christ pastor in Big Spring, Texas, David Tarbet, placed a display ad in his local newspaper in 1964[260] in response to Allen's healing claims.

In that ad, Tarbet said that he had been recently offended when he was driving down a Texas highway and heard Allen on his car radio. Target did not actually name Allen, but referred to "the folk at Miracle Valley" in his ad. Tarbet referred to Allen as saying,

God is not coming back for a sick church. Jesus came to set the captives free! Sickness is bondage. If you want to be among the redeemed church at the judgment you must be without blemish - and that means without sickness in body.

Tarbet did not say that this was a direct quote, although quotation marks were used. Instead, he said that this was what he heard on the radio, "in effect."

He seemed especially bothered by this statement because of something he read into it. In Tarbet's interpretation, this statement meant that "one will go to hell for sickness of the body as soon as for sickeness [sic] of the soul."

Whether Allen would have interpreted the statement in the same way is another matter. Still, however, Tarbet was offended.

"Where does the Bible make any such statement?" he asked. Tarbet added,

Where does the Bible say Jesus came to free all men held captive by physical illness? Where is the verse that teaches that Jesus died on the cross to redeem all men from physical disease?

Those who believe in divine healing through the name of Jesus could, no doubt, have quoted any one of a number of scriptural reference for Tarbet's benefit. Matthew 8:16-17 says, for example, that Jesus " . . . healed all who were sick, so that it could be fulfilled which was spoken by Isaiah the prophet, saying Himself took our infirmities and bore our sicknesses." Similarly, 1 Peter 2:24 asserts that he, " . . . his own self bore our sins in his own body on the tree, so that we, being dead to sins, should live to righteousness, by whose stripes we were healed."

Still, Tarbet was hard-pressed to come up with a single verse. He did manage, however, to point out that 2 Timothy 4:20 refers to Paul having left Trophimus ill at Miletus. He also cited Paul asking the Lord to "heal his own infirmity," saying that "the Lord refused," citing 2 Corinthians 12:7-9.

While David Tarbet does not directly mention Allen in his ad, the implication is clear. Before he closed with a tag line which reads that "The Church of Christ welcomes you," he ended his questions on divine healing with "Maybe the folk at 'Miracle Valley' have an answer. We shall see."

This matter of Paul's "thorn in the flesh" was directly addressed in one of Allen's study courses. Although it is not clear whether Allen himself wrote the section dealing with the subject, since other ministry associates assisted with writing his course materials,[261] A.A. Allen made certain this subject was addressed in his Lesson No. 3 of his "Health-Healing-Holiness" study course. This course was a part of Allen's "Preministerial and Christian Workers' Bible College Correspondence Courses."[262]

The course quotes from the same passage that Tarbet had raised in his newspaper display ad, 2 Corinthians 12:7-9. The concept that this "thorn" was some form of sickness is then countered, however, by asserting that

Yet to say that Paul's thorn was a physical defect would certainly require some backing beyond what is found in this passage of Scripture, for sickness is not mentioned. The strongest advocates of the idea that the thorn was a physical weakness dare not go further than to say, "It has been conjectured that Paul's thorn in the flesh was chronic ophthalmia" (severe inflammation of the eyes).

In referring to this idea, the course refers to a note in the Schofield reference Bible. The course further points out that,

Surely in the face of the glorious promises of healing given boldly in the Word of God, something stronger than a mere conjecture that Paul was sick should be required to cancel such strong promises.

The course then refers to two of the scriptures mentioned above, Joshua 23:13 and Judges 2:3, as providing evidence that the "thorn" concept refers "not to something within the body, but to annoyances from without, caused by people."

In addition, one meaning of the word "buffet" is explained as being "to contend with." Significant evidence that the "thorn" does not refer to sickness comes from another point:

In the list of the infirmities in which Paul chooses to glory (2 Cor. 11:23-33), there is no sickness, nor blindness mentioned, but rather persecutions. He does mention weariness and painfulness, but would not beatings, stonings, hunger, and cold be sufficient cause for weariness and painfulness?

The course added,

Careful consideration of the words used by Paul, by comparing those words with their accepted definition and the manner in which they are used in other Scriptures, would indicate that Paul's thorn in the flesh was something from without, probably his treatment by other persons or another person. His reference to 'buffeting' would refer more easily to the beatings, stonings, and the like which he received after he preached the Gospel from city to city, than to any possible sickness in his own body.

Added to this is the fact that in Paul's own writings are found many of the tremendous promises of healing.

David Tarbet placed his newspaper ad in January of 1964, challenging Allen's beliefs about healing. In October of that year, A.A. Allen's ministry had come to Torrance in the Los Angeles area for a "New Restoration Revival." Allen's tent was set up off of the Harbor Freeway (today Interstate 110) at the Torrance Boulevard exit. This was a short distance south of the San Diego Freeway (today I-405).

For years, one or another evangelist had claimed to be ministering from the "world's largest" gospel tent. An ad promoting the Torrance meeting proclaimed that the Allen meetings were being conducted not in the world's largest tent, but in the world's "greatest" gospel tent.[263]

An added inducement to attend was the statement that TV cameras would be "filming each evening." Joy, healing, peace, "new life" (the born-again experience), and the "power to get wealth" were being restored, according to the ad. The ad, however, said that this was all "according to the Bible (Joel 1)."

Before coming to Torrance, Allen had ministered in Chicago in July of the same year, 1964. His Chicago meetings were held in the Coliseum. In response to criticism, an ad for those meetings, which appeared in the *Chicago Defender*, urged potential guests to ignore public remarks directed against Allen and his ministry:

DON'T BE DECEIVED BY PROPAGANDA!

DON'T BE MISLED BY "POISON PEN" WRITERS!

Further,

DON'T LET RUSSIA BRAINWASH YOU IN A CHURCH WASH PAN![264]

Yet another controversy regarding Allen and Miracle Valley struck in 1964 when 17 indictments were issued by a grand jury in an investigation of theft of money contained in letters sent to Miracle Valley. The press revealed that one involved a local postal employee who stole $5 out of a letter addressed to the ministry.

Details of other such incidents were kept secret, but could have involved much more significant amounts.[265] In January of the following year, 1965, an assistant postmaster pleaded guilty to a charge of delaying mail. This was after he was accused of removing a letter addressed to Miracle Valley from a mail pouch.[266]

Also in 1965, another Miracle Valley controversy surfaced when a local school board complained that its schools were overcrowded and undersupported, and that this was the fault of "the Miracle Valley religious settlement headed by Allen."[267] The board of Palominas School, southwest of Miracle Valley, complained that 55% of its 105 students came from the "religious settlement," and that Miracle Valley was "not meeting its share" of the costs of running the school. The claim was advanced that this was a result of the 1963 federal tax court ruling in favor of Miracle Valley.[268]

The board claimed that overcrowding at the school had reached crisis proportions, and that A.A. Allen was the cause. Palominas School, it was said, was built with about 25 students and one teacher in mind. Now its student population had sprung to 105, with four teachers to serve them.

The president of the school board said that 55% of those students came from Miracle Valley.[269] If 55% of 105 students were associated with Miracle Valley, that would be around 58 students. One thing that the school board president did not mention is that even without the presence of students from Miracle Valley, the school was attempting to accommodate about 47 students, or nearly double its intended occupancy.

The school board claimed that it had no money to expand. Allen's brother in law Gerald W. King, executive director of Miracle Valley, represented Allen's ministry at a public meeting. King said that $4,531 had been paid the previous year by the Allen ministry and by residents of Miracle Valley.

Around the same time, Dale Davis, who ministered extensively with the Allen ministry at Miracle Valley, said that he attempted to send his two children to the Palominas School, but was told that they would not be admitted. Davis submitted a motion for a writ of mandamus before a judge of the Cochise County Superior Court, but his request was denied. A writ of mandamus orders a government official to perform an action which that official is required to do, but which has been neglected.

The judge said that the school had not denied admission to Davis's children. Instead, he said, the school board would make a decision after a hearing to determine the children's residency.[270]

If this wasn't enough, the Southern Pacific Railroad made changes in its local lines. As a result, although the railroad had been paying $31,000 a year in school taxes, now only about $10,000 could be expected.[271]

By 1969, however, the tax situation had shifted, if a letter from Frank C. Adams to a Phoenix paper is any indication. Adams, who was clerk of the Palominas School Board of Trustees. Adams objected to an earlier news report which claimed that Palominas was overcrowded because of Allen and his ministry, and that Allen's followers were not paying their fair share of taxes.

On the contrary, according to Adams, those associated with Allen's ministry were taxed at the same rate as everyone else. Further, he noted, Allen's ministry organization was the "only employer that pays any tax to amount to much" as far as the school's support was concerned.

He cited the district's three major employers as being the U.S. Army, Phelps Dodge Corporation, and A.A. Allen Revivals, Inc., presumably in that order. Adams noted that the Army didn't pay taxes and that the holdings of Phelps-Dodge were, as he put it, "mostly" outside of the district associated with the Palominas School.[272]

Another controversy centered around talk of raising the dead. At one point during the 1960s, Allen and others at Miracle Valley began speaking of a desire for faith to even raise the dead. This was misinterpreted by outsiders as an effort by Allen to expand influence and income by claiming this power.

One later observer, for instance, claimed that Allen "launched his 'Raise the Dead' campaign," and appears to have historically misplaced his move as a mid-1950s event. That writer further refers to this as representing "a faith . . . that verges on the deranged."[273]

The claim was made that Allen was "forced to discontinue this mission"[274] when corpses were sent to Miracle Valley with the aim of having them resurrected. Sending the dead to Miracle Valley was said to have "verged on the deranged," but, of course, Allen was personally blamed.

Associates of Allen at Miracle Valley

By 1964, A.A. Allen was personally ministering in Latin America, a practice which resulted in several "missionary films." In 1964, he had "just returned from overseas," where "record breaking multitudes" had attended his services in the West Indies and in South America.[275]

Not only was A.A. Allen himself engaged in a healing ministry, but others associated with his ministry, including graduates of the Bible college at Miracle Valley, were also engaged in healing. When a healing revival involving Rev. Sara Steward was advertised in 1964 in Lebanon, Pennsylvania, for instance, it was noted that she was "From the A.A. Allen Miracle Valley Arizona School." Like Allen, she too was claiming that "God works miracles thru her ministry."[276]

Similarly, when in 1966 meetings were held in Hobbs, New Mexico, featuring evangelist C.Y. Kelly, Allen's wording was borrowed when the campaign was termed a "restoration revival." Kelly was to preach a sermon called "Miracles, Signs and Wonders Being Wrought in these Last and Evil Days" in a church pastored by G.B. Morgan. According to Morgan, his church was a "branch" of Allen's Miracle Revival Fellowship.[277]

In the same year, a California evangelist, Robert Larry, was referred to by the press as "a prophet of the Miracle Valley Revival Center in California." Obviously Arizona was meant. Larry was holding a "Holy Ghost Miracle revival" for a Pentecostal Holiness church at Glen Raven, North Carolina.[278]

Yet another evangelist who ministered outside of Miracle Valley yet claimed Miracle Valley associations was Spurgeon O'Donnell. A 1968 mention of his appearance as a guest revivalist refers to O'Donnell as a "successful evangelist" involved in traveling ministry in the western U.S. He was described as "a former pastor of Miracle Valley Arizona church."[279]

Various Christian musical artists also visited Miracle Valley and ministered from time to time from the platform. Among the best-remembered were Nancy Harmon, the Statesmen Quartet, and Goldia Haynes.

Goldia Haynes is considered one of the all-time legends of gospel music. When she ministered in El Paso in 1968, she was advertised as "The Nationally Known Gospel Singer and Evangelist" with her party from East St. Louis, Illinois. They were said to have just returned from Miracle Valley, "where they have been working, preaching and singing for the Internationally Known Evangelist Rev. A.A. Allen."

In that event and at Miracle Valley, Goldia Hayes was accompanied by her son, an accomplished gospel pianist and organized, Sylvester Haynes. Those promoting the 1968 revival services were confident that manifestations of the supernatural power of God would be present:

> Evangelist Haynes is a woman who God has given a great message and who God is using to bring deliverance to multitudes. There will be signs, wonders and miracles each night.[280]

Paul J. Cunningham, who had been serving as a foreign missionary, became associated with the Allen ministry in the role of a prophet, beginning in 1965. According to Cunningham's own testimony, he had been holding revival meetings in Vallejo, California at the Veterans Memorial Auditorium in February 1965. That was when he experienced an unusual event in his apartment.

As he told the story, he had gone to bed about 1:30 in the morning after what he described as "a tremendous outpouring of the Spirit of God" in his revival service. As he explained,

> At about 2 am, the room filled with light, and suspecting that someone had entered and turned on the light, I sat up in bed and looked around. The room was empty of any human being, but filled with a glorious, supernatural light, and in the midst of the light stood an angel of God.

That angel, according to Cunningham, then directed him to go to Miracle Valley. He was given words to deliver to A.A. Allen, and was told to go at once:

> The angel spoke: "Fear not: I am sent of God to instruct you and tell you of a new move of God that is beginning in the earth. . . . This move will be called restoration revival, and will bring restoration to the church, the body of Christ, and will be different from any other revival the world has ever known, as it will climax with the physical return of Jesus Christ."

He was further instructed,

> "You are to close your crusade here in Vallejo and go to Miracle Valley, Arizona to minister to A.A. Allen. These are the words you are to tell him: 'God has chosen you to spearhead and announce restoration revival to the world. You will be used of God to begin this new move, which will continue until Christ returns. You will need new faith to take a new step forward. This will be granted unto you and your ministry will grow by leaps and bounds, because the world must hear, and you have been chosen by God to announce it to them.'"

Finally, he told was told, "Go to Miracle Valley and you will be given further instruction. Go at once."[281]

Three days after Cunningham arrived at Miracle Valley, he was able to speak with Allen. As Allen was prostrated in the Spirit with his arms raised aloft, Paul J. Cunningham prophesied over him. A small photo of the event was published in the April 1965 issue of Allen's *Miracle Magazine* with the following caption:

> Prophecy came forth to Brother Allen as ministers prayed for his special anointing, " . . . surely thou shalt find within thee, yea, the faith and the power to arise and step forth! And the Lord, thy God, shall walk beside thee, and thou shalt not step alone, but the Lord, thy God shall be with thee holding thy hand, lifting thy feet, and thou shalt not stagger nor falter nor fail . . . ."[282]

As Paul J. Cunningham later explained, "for the next 6 years (until his death in 1970), I was the prophet to the Allen ministry and a close personal friend of A.A. Allen's." He added, "I ate at the same table with him, often slept in the same motels, was in many of the revival meetings he conducted across America, and was his 'agent' in the UK." He also, according to his testimony, served as an "invited guest speaker" twice a year at all of the Miracle Valley camp meetings from then on, until Allen's death.[283]

Cunningham did, however, continue to hold his own meetings. In 1969, for instance, he held meetings in Ada, Oklahoma. A display ad promoted him and his ministry as "the internationally famous 20th century prophet and a great evangelistic team." Borrowing from Allen's approach, the ad proclaimed that a "mighty restoration revival campaign" would be held, with "Signs! Wonders! Healings! Miracles!"

In addition, the "secrets of men's hearts" were to be "revealed by the Spirit of God." The ad included a statement from A.A. Allen which seems enigmatic in the light of Cunningham's statements about involvement with Allen's ministry:

Although Rev. Cunningham Is Not Associated or Connected with A.A. Allen Revivals, Inc., We Feel Sure You Will be Blessed by His Anointed Ministry. - A.A. ALLEN.[284]

Perhaps all that was meant, however, was simply that Cunningham's meetings were being conducted separately from Allen and Miracle Valley. A news item from later the same year, when he was holding revival meetings in a Foursquare church, referred to him as "Evangelist Paul J. Cunningham from Hamilton, Tex."[285]

Of course, Cunningham was close to various individuals at Miracle Valley, but one he mentioned in particular as a friend was Jennie Evans. She appears in some of Allen's TV programs as an older woman in the choir.

At one point, choir members form what Pentecostals used to call a "Jericho march," as they streamed down from the choir and up the aisle of the tabernacle at Miracle Valley. Evans noticeably held up the line as she attempted her descent from the platform, presumably due to her age.

Jennie Evans was born in 1902, according to her tombstone in the Miracle Valley Cemetery. She died in 1968, two years before the death of A.A. Allen.[286] Ironically, one of the most significant figures in the well-known Azusa Street revival of 1906 was Jennie Evans Moore.

By 1965, ministry associate Don Stewart was being prominently featured in Allen advertising as a "dynamic evangelist."[287] He ministered in Allen's meetings along with H. Kent Rogers. Music was being provided by singer Gene Martin, organist David Davis, and pianist T. C. Anderson.

By 1966, Claude Sheldon ("C.S.") Upthegrove, an evangelist, was advertising that he had been associated with A.A. Allen, serving as pastor of the church at Miracle Valley. In fact, he ran advertising that featured the name of A.A. Allen in huge letters with his own name in relatively tiny lettering.[288] Even today, the C. S. Upthegrove website refers to his service as "former pastor of Miracle Valley Church under the late Brother AA Allen" as the first specific claim to fame mentioned.[289]

Upthegrove was born in 1923 in Okeechobee, Florida. His website refers to him as "one of the last remaining of God's Generals of the Ladder [sic; Latter] Rain movement of the 1950s and 60s."[290] As has already been noted, however, A.A. Allen distanced himself from the Latter Rain movement.

Allen named Upthegrove as the pastor of the church at Miracle Valley in 1965.

In one of Allen's meetings at Miracle Valley, he announced that,

> Prayer has been going up to heaven as to who would be the pastor of this great international miracle revival center. And God answered prayer yesterday and the Holy Ghost spoke in his own way and told us what to do about this. And I'm about to introduce the new pastor of Miracle Valley Revival - International, shall I say - Revival Center, and who is also going to be very instrumental in seeing that you and your loved ones receive

your healing because hundreds of people here and thousands around the world are going to be praying day and night that God will send the angel to trouble the waters for your healing.

So the pastor of Miracle Valley Bible Training Center and Miracle Valley International Revival Center, Bethesda Healing Faith Clinic is none other than Rev. C. S. Upthegrove from West Palm Beach, Florida . . . . [291]

Allen added that, "This is the man whom God has sent, Brother Upthegrove." That was 1965.[292] By the following year, however, Upthegrove was advertising that he was "formerly Pastor, Miracle Valley, Ariz. with A.A. Allen." Still, "Visible Miracles - Healing - Power" were to be expected from his meetings.[293]

Upthegrove was evidently resuming a practice he had pursued before serving at Miracle Valley. In 1963, for example, he was holding tent revival meetings billed as "voice of deliverance crusade salvation and healing services." At that time, he was being referred to as a "radio evangelist."[294]

In addition to Upthegrove, another minister who had become closely associated with Allen and Miracle Valley by this time was a fiery young evangelist named Dale Davis. When Davis appeared at a "Big Gospel Tent Salvation Deliverance Revival" in Gastonia, North Carolina, in 1966, he was referred to as "America's Restoration Revival Evangelist."[295] By 1969, he was said to be "known for his missionary, revival, and TV work."[296]

Various ministries which had been associated with Allen and Miracle Valley at one time or another continued to minister, oftentimes with reference to Allen in their newspaper display ads. One of those ads noted that even the Miracle Valley Choir was ministering on its own, in a church in Phoenix in 1969.[297]

Individuals who had been ministering in some capacity at Miracle Valley often went out on their own, using their relationship with Miracle Valley and Allen's ministry as a means of boosting promotion. In 1969, for instance, Clarine Westerby, who had been Dean of Girls at Miracle Valley Bible College, was ministering on her own as an evangelist. Advertising pointed to her former position at Miracle Valley.[298]

Chapter 6:

A Media Ministry

Still, Allen revival meetings in other cities continued. In 1965, an Allen "New Restoration Revival" came to Corpus Christi, Texas, scheduled for September 22 through 29. Tommy C. Anderson ministered each morning on the gifts and operation of the Holy Spirit. In the afternoons, H. Kent Rogers spoke, and prayer cards were distributed.

This appears to have been a typical approach. When a "Summer Campmeeting" was held in Baltimore in 1963, Anderson taught each morning on "operation of Holy Ghost and gifts of the Spirit." H. Kent Rogers would be holding "Faith Clinic Services" in the afternoons, when prayer line cards would be distributed.[299]

Tommy C. Anderson was probably far better known as Allen's piano player, and H. Kent Rogers commonly led singing in some of Allen's meetings. An ad for the Corpus Christi meetings referred to Rogers as the "world's foremost song leader."

Then, in the evening, was scheduled a "Great EVANGELISTIC RALLY with 'God's Man of Faith' praying for the sick and afflicted."[300] The prayer cards which had been distributed during the day served several purposes: They determined who would receive prayer that evening, they provided Allen with a written description of each individual's ailments or infirmities, and they insured that those who came for prayer had received instruction earlier in the day in how to receive by faith.

As usual, music would be provided by Gene Martin, advertised as "one of the greatest gospel singers of all time." He was to be accompanied by "various musical groups."[301]

Before the Corpus Christi meetings were over, Allen was already using similar ads to promote another "New Restoration Revival," this time in El Paso, scheduled at Liberty Hall September 29 and 30, as well as October 2 and 3. Details of those meetings were announced in terms nearly identical to those in Corpus Christi.[302]

One additional feature in El Paso newspaper advertising, however, was reference to his radio program, "The Allen Revival Hour." This program could be heard over a Mexican "border blaster" radio station:

HEAR "The Allen Revival Hour" DAILY Radio Broadcast

Juarez, Mexico

XELO, 520 kc, 7:45 p.m.

Ft. Worth, Texas

XEG, 1050 kc, 8:15 p.m.[303]

As has already been noted, Allen's broadcasts had appeared on XELO as early as 1955. XELO was one of several mostly English-language radio stations which were based in Mexico and intended for American audiences. The popularity of these stations to ministries and to some advertisers were obvious: The Mexico-based "border blasters" could exceed American legal power limits while, at times, evading American laws as to advertised products.

XELO in particular was created by an American, Will Branch, who had established several such border radio stations. Allen was not the only minister using such stations. The presence of American preachers on XELO began in the 1940s, and by 1971 the station's annual billings for religious programs in English amounted to over $170,000.[304]

Around the mid-1960s, while other evangelists were asking individuals to lay their hands on the radio as a point of contact, Allen was sending out life-size photos of his hands. As promoted in Allen's Miracle Magazine,

> Peter's shadow brought healing to a multitude! This life size photo of my hands sent free, anywhere, upon request. You may use convenient blank at right.[305]

Around this time, Allen's radio program was being carried on at least two Mexican stations, XERB and XEG.[306] XERB, in particular, was one of the best remembered Mexican stations known as "border blasters." These radio stations broadcast in English into the United States, but were situated in Mexico, enabling them to avoid U.S. power limitations. So-called border blasters became known for their tendency to sometimes feature dubious broadcasters and advertising, not all of which would have been allowed on American stations.

In later years XERB became infamously associated with legendary disc jockey Wolfman Jack. XEG's broadcasts emanated from Monterey, and XERB was located in Rosarito Beach, near Tijuana.

Allen and Prosperity

A.A. Allen sometimes taught on Biblical promises of financially prosperity, although this was certainly never a dominant theme in his ministry. A 1968 book published by his ministry was a study by Allen on this subject, titled *God's Guarantee to Bless and Prosper You Financially*. The book was subtitled *God's Divine Plan to Put an End to Poverty*.

The cover of that book quotes from several scriptural passages which outline Allen's views on the subject. Among those scriptures are the following:

Deuteronomy Chapter 8:18: But thou shalt remember the Lord thy God: for it is he that giveth thee power to get wealth.

Psalms Chapter 112: Praise ye the Lord. Blessed is the man that feareth the Lord, that delighteth greatly in his commandments. Wealth and riches shall be in his house: and his righteousness endureth for ever. . . .

Deuteronomy Chapter 28:11: And the Lord shall make thee plenteous in goods, ... [307]

In this book, Allen noted that, for him, Ecclesiastes 5:19 made it especially clear that God wants his people to financially prosper. That scripture reads,

> Every man also to whom God hath given riches and wealth, and hath given him power to eat thereof, and to take his portion, and to rejoice in his labour; this is the gift of God.

He added that

> if there was not another scripture in the Bible, Eccl. 5:19 is enough to let me know that God wants to give me this gift, which is the gift of prosperity.[308]

Allen's Last Full Year of Ministry

By 1969, which would prove to be A.A. Allen's last full year of ministry, he was certainly high profile, while still just as controversial. Both *Time* and *Look* magazines featured major articles on the man, using the journalistic approach one would expect.

The article in *Time* claimed that Allen would retaliate with "fiery recriminations" directed against pastors who would "release" individuals from financial pledges to Allen's ministry.[309] On the other hand, *Look* noted in its headline that with regard to claims of healing in Allen's services, "He Heals," insinuating that Allen personally claimed the power to heal. At the same time, the gospel music present in Allen's tent was, to a *Look* reporter, characterized by a "pelvic beat."[310]

Plenty of emphasis was placed on the amount of money coming into the ministry. Of course, little or no attention in either article was placed on the amount of money flowing out of the ministry in terms of expenses.

The *Time* article noted that not just last year, but last year "alone," Allen's ministry organization "grossed $2,692,342 - not counting the salaries of Allen and his two associate preachers, who take their cut directly from 'their ministry.'" Where the magazine thought they should have "taken their cuts" from, or what the ministry's expenses were, are factors which are not mentioned.

A *Time* reporter noted in the first paragraph the racially integrated nature of Allen's services. The second paragraph emphasizes Allen's supposedly flamboyant nature, with reference to what was termed his "usual iridescent lavender suit."[311]

The article notes the absence of that suit in a particular service, but without making it clear why it was expected, or to what extent it constituted Allen's "usual." Most surviving Allen TV programs are in black and white. The few remaining and circulating color programs do not appear to provide evidence of a lavender suit.

Look magazine, during the same year, referred to Allen as resembling "a garish leprechaun" in what was described as a "camel-colored" suit with a yellow shirt and orange tie.[312] No mention was made of any "usual" lavender suit. The "garish" reference would have to refer to the shirt and tie, not the suit, but this was, after all, the late '60s, when "garish" styles were, to a large extent, the norm.

Accounts are given in that article of dramatic claims of healing, accounts which must have seemed far-fetched to uninitiated readers who only learned of them from brief quotes by Allen. Throughout the article, Allen's ministry is made to seem flashy and based on exaggeration, with Allen directly referred to as "the star" of A.A. Allen Revivals, Inc.

The article notes that one person claimed to have received supernatural fillings in her teeth, while someone else received new disks in his spine. The intended insinuation is clear when the article then quotes from Allen's *Miracle Magazine*: "A.A. Allen Revivals, Inc. assumes no legal responsibility for the veracity of any such reports."

A 1969 newspaper description of Miracle Valley focused on the "huge church" with its great dome of red, blue, and gold. Made of plexiglas, the dome was described as the prayer tower for the church at Miracle Valley, which was said to seat 3,500. According to the paper, the dome was "visible for miles."[313] That seems echoed by recent claims that the dome is used as a sort of way marker for illegal aliens entering the U.S. from past the very close Mexican border.

Another description noted that the sign which arched over the entrance to Miracle Valley seemed out of place and a bit overly "grand" considering its rural environment. The sign read "A.A. Allen Revivals Inc., International Headquarters." That was only because of the sign's rural environment, it was said.[314] It would not be because of Allen's reputation. By this time, everyone, it would seem, had at least heard of A.A. Allen.

Allen's ministry headquarters at the time sat on a 2,400-acre tract between Bisbee and Ft. Huachuca. This was on Arizona State Route 92, which runs entirely in Cochise County. Miracle Valley was home to a cattle ranch, farm, and orchards apparently designed to aid in self-sufficiency. A landing strip and, of course, housing for students, employees, and permanent residents, were also vital components of the Miracle Valley community.

Perhaps as an attempt to boost Miracle Valley's image among the locals, a display ad appeared in a Tucson newspaper in 1969 announcing the "Annual Commencement Exercises" of Miracle Valley Bible College. The ad, which featured a drawing of a graduate in traditional cap and gown, noted that this was an "ALL WELCOME" event to be held at Miracle Valley Church.

As though no one in the Tucson area knew who was Allen was, the same ad proclaimed that "National Known Evangelist A.A. Allen, Founder and President of the College, will give the Commencement Address." This was to be a two-day event, with a baccalaureate service one day and the commencement the next.[315]

A 1969 report noted that, in the previous year, Allen's ministry grossed more than $2.6 million.[316] The paper said nothing about expenditures except to note that the payroll was "about $850,000." This was according to Gerald King, Miracle Valley's operations manager.

About 350,000[317] or 400,000[318] copies of Allen's *Miracle Magazine* were being mailed out at the time, apparently without charging a subscription fee. According to Paul J. Cunningham, who worked as a prophet and missions director with the Allen ministry, the magazine's circulation was about 500,000 during its last two years, with a pass-along readership of 2.5 million.[319]

Another paper around the same time quoted similar circulation figures, while calling Miracle Valley Allen's "religion factory, moneyhouse, and spiritual revival center." Gerald King's wife Leeta (listed in the 1910 census as Leattie), who was A.A. Allen's sister, answered the phone and opened mail from behind a glass window in the lobby of the administration building.[320]

Miracle Valley operated its own print shop and record factory. In the record plant, Miracle Valley produced a number of phonograph records of primarily music by the ministry's choir, musicians, and singers, as well as an occasional record of preaching by Allen. These were sold at meetings and were offered by Allen in his television programs. This record-producing facility was described as "one of the finest sound recording laboratories in the state."[321]

The ministry also produced a regular output of radio broadcasts, distributed on reel-to-reel tape, as well as films, most of which were intended for use as half-hour television programs. In 1969, Miracle Valley's volume of incoming mail was estimated at about 60 million pieces a year.[322]

Students attending Miracle Valley's Bible College went through a nine-month course while living in dormitories on campus. The campus also included a dining hall.

In 1969, Allen was said to be leading a "flock" of about 3,000. That was when a group which, by its own admission, was a satanic cult, mailed a strangely worded threat to Allen: "Unless you join us, a giant cavern will open beneath Miracle Valley and everyone in Miracle Valley will be swallowed up."[323]

When Allen died in 1970, his ministry organization was operating Bible schools at not only Miracle Valley, but in the Philippines as well. The organization was employing 175 persons.[324] Miracle Valley was being referred to as "a bustling little town" with "computerized office buildings and a 3,500-seat temple with a multicolored dome."[325]

In spite of the extensive operations of Allen's ministry organization at Miracle Valley, he was still traveling around the country conducting revival crusades up to the time that he died in 1970. In 1968, for example, he applied to erect a 300-foot tent in San Leandro, California,[326] an application which was approved. There his ministry held three services a day, two on Sunday.[327]

Allen's tent was said to house about 4,000 folding chairs in 1969.[328] A semi truck followed Allen to revival services across the country, and was reported as late as April of 1970 to be racking up over 100,000 miles a year.

The truck bore huge letters on the side which read "A.A. Allen. Salvation healing. Miracle revivals. Television - Allen Revival Hour - Radio, international headquarters, Miracle Valley, Ariz."[329] The truck was used to carry "an organ, a piano, loudspeakers, elaborate tape-recording equipment" used for radio programs, plus boxes of books and records to be sold at Allen's meetings.[330]

An article in the *New York Times* that reported Allen's death noted that he had been still using a "huge tent."[331] Outside the tent, visitors were met by signs which read,

A.A. ALLEN REVIVALS, INC., MIRACLE VALLEY, ARIZ. The Blind to See, The Deaf to Hear, The Lame to Walk. SIGNS. GIFTS. WONDERS.

When proper facilities could be found, however, Allen meetings were held in stadiums, coliseums, and arenas. A September 1969 series of meetings in Richmond, Virginia, for example, were held in a local arena.[332] Services in December of that year were conducted in the Chicago Coliseum.[333]

Healing was still being ministered, although Allen often relied on "miracle music" through Gene Martin and others, rather than his personal "laying on of hands," to accomplish this. "I never healed anybody," Allen was quoted[334] as saying. "God heals them. I just pray. I encourage people to come and worship God. Healing's just a bonus."

The *Times* also quoted Allen as noting that Allen was still in the fray even after the era of tent revivalism had essentially closed.

> There are no evangelists left that offer us any competition. We've got the field. Back in the late '40s and '50s, Jack Coe, Oral Roberts, O. L. Jaggers and 200 others, you know, there were 200 evangelists all praying for the sick, having healing revivals. Now they're nonexistent.

The same paper reported that, with regard to his approach, Allen claimed he was optimistic about the future. Allen was quoted as saying that many were dissatisfied with the "cold, dead hand of denominationalism."

This was at a time when two major revival movements - the Charismatic Movement and the Jesus Movement - were coalescing. The two movements would combine would prevail through the early '70s, would wane by the early '80s, and would leave in their wake huge "megachurches" by the early '90s.

Oral Roberts, who at one time was undoubtedly the best known tent-revival-oriented healing evangelist, was said to have "dropped out and turned Methodist" by 1969, as far as healing meetings were concerned.[335] That wording appeared in *Look* magazine in that year, and earlier the same year, *Time* noted that Roberts had "joined the Methodist ministry and de-emphasized the curative aspects of his high-decibel revivals."[336] Allen, by contrast, kept going.

Chapter 7:

The Death of A.A. Allen

A.A. Allen died quite unexpectedly and at the age of only 59. A number of news articles focused on what was termed a "strange coincidence,"[337] a quirk in scheduling. That "strange coincidence" resulted in radio stations across the country airing a recorded Allen radio program immediately after his death, in which he spoke out against rumors that he had died:[338]

> This is Brother Allen in person. Numbers of friends of mine have been inquiring about reports they have heard concerning me that are not true. People as well as some preachers from pulpits are announcing that I am dead.

> Do I sound like a dead man? My friends, I am not even sick. Only a moment ago I made reservations to fly into our current campaign where I'll see you there and make the devil a liar.

Those reservations may have been for revival meetings in Pittsburgh. A ticket was found among Allen's belongings in his hotel room right after he died. That ticket was referred to in the coroner's report as a "Pittsburgh-S.F." ticket.

Newspaper headlines across the country reported that he had died of acute alcoholism, as though this was incontrovertible. Later, numerous other sources referred to his death as having been the result of alcoholism, as though this claim was an established fact.

Heilbut, in his book *The Gospel Sound*, for instance, matter-of-factly says that Allen "died recently of alcoholism."[339] Typically, newspaper headlines were anything but subtle in their statements:

- "Alcoholism Said Cause of Allen's Death" (*Altoona Mirror*, Altoona, PA)[340]

- "Alcoholism Took Life of Evangelist Allen" (*Daily Report*, Ontario-Upland, CA)[341]

- "Allen Preached Temperance, Died of Alcoholism" (*Arizona Republic*, Phoenix)[342]

- "Evangelist Dies of Alcoholism" (*Daily Review*, Hayward, CA)[343]

- "Evangelist's Death Laid to Alcoholism" (*Bridgeport Telegram*, Bridgeport, CT)[344]

Some later writers were even less kind. In her book *Global Pentecostal and Charismatic Healing*, Candy Gunther Brown asserts that he "struggled all his life from alcoholism and died from cirrhosis of the liver."[345] No documentation is provided for the statement that he "struggled all his life" with alcoholism.

Similarly, Randall Balmer, in his *Encyclopedia of Evangelicalism*,[346] refers to "the persistent rumors" of Allen's drinking prior to the so-called "Knoxville Incident," again without offering documentation. If there were such rumors, perhaps they stemmed in part from his own testimony regarding his pre-Christian life.

The claim of David Harrel in his book *All Things Are Possible*[347] that Allen "tottered constantly on the brink of psychological collapse" (again, without footnote) has done nothing to mitigate the belief that Allen was a troubled alcoholic. Harrell also refers to Allen's "turbulent personality"[348] with no direct explanation or immediate reference citation.

Again, such comments may stem from A.A. Allen's candid testimony of the nature of his life before his conversion. Harrell does quote Allen as having said, for example, that by the age of 21, he was, in his own words, "a nervous wreck. . . . I was a confirmed drunkard."

This is, however, referring to his earlier life. Certainly Allen was controversial, and he stepped on people's toes. Was Allen's testimony commonly used by a number of his detractors as a basis to construct an overall negative evaluation of his life and ministry? If so, could this view have found its way into later accounts?

Harrell[349] refers to Allen as a "radical," and says that during the mid-'50s "intense pressure was applied" to "isolate" such radical ministries as those of Allen and another prominent Voice of Healing minister, Jack Coe. To some extent, that does appear to be true. Both Jack Coe and A.A. Allen were, on separate occasions, the subjects of negative evaluations by the Assemblies of God organization.

Ministry associate Paul J. Cunningham discussed what he knew of Allen's death. In his narrative, he refers to Bernie Schwartz, who Cunningham said in an interview had been Allen's "radio agent." According to Cunningham, Allen was in San Francisco in order to meet with Schwartz and Allen's brother-in-law Gerald King in order to deal with radio contracts.

Allen had been suffering with extreme knee pain. Allen, according to Cunningham, said that he was feeling very tired, and went to his room early. Later, someone called his room and was unable to get him to respond.

That person had the hotel unlock Allen's door, and Allen was found dead. No alcohol bottles were in the room.[350] In a written statement, Cunningham gives his take on what transpired:[351]

> I spoke with Bro. Allen by telephone, from England, just a few days prior to his death. He told me he was "going to San Francisco, with Gerald King (his brother in law, and executive director) to meet with Burney Schwartz, to re-do the radio contracts." (The Allen Revival Hour was then carried on about 186 stations daily.)

> I returned to the US and a couple of days later, he died. I spoke with Gerald King, and others; read the Medical Examiners report, and was also an "honor guard" at his funeral.

> According to Gerald King and Bernie Schwartz, " We were in the Jack Tar Hotel in S.F. in the late afternoon, and Bro. Allen said, Boys, I feel tired, I believe I'll rest a bit, before we go to dinner." Bernie said, "I went to my room, and about 8 p.m. began to be concerned, because I hadn't heard from Allen." "I phoned his room, got no reply, so went up and knocked on the door, and still got

no reply." "I then proceeded to get the manager, and he opened the door, and we found Bro. Allen slumped over in an easy chair, dead."

The medical Examiner issued a certificate of death, stating the cause of death as "an apparent heart attack."

Many stories have been told, some stating that "the room was full of empty liquor bottles," and others, that he "died an alcoholic"....but they are all lies, based on "narrow minded, evil surmisings," by people who would rather discredit the ministry, than to "believe the truth."

More illuminating is the coroner's report.[352] That report starts out, however, by simply noting the obvious: A 160-pound, 5-foot-9 white man with red hair and brown eyes was found dead in Room 418 of the Jack Tar Hotel. He was employed by the Miracle Valley Bible College in Miracle Valley, Arizona, where his "usual occupation" was that of "President."

According to the report, A.A. Allen registered at the hotel, located at 1101 Van Ness Avenue, at 12:56 pm on June 11th. According to various online comments about the property, the hotel was, at one time, highly regarded, but eventually, long after Allen's death, had fallen into decline.

The coroner's report noted that Bernard Schwartz, who Cunningham called Bernie Schwartz, was "a friend of the deceased." Schwartz, according to the report, called Allen about 9:15 in the evening. As a result of the call, Schwartz became "alarmed," and contacted the hotel's assistant manager.

Schwartz and the assistant manager then went to Allen's room. When there was no response to their knocking, they entered the room with a pass key and found Allen dead, sitting in front of the television.

The coroner's report noted that when the coroner arrived, Allen was lying on the bed, where emergency personnel had placed him, wearing only his underwear. "Old surgical scars" were seen on his left knee, the result of a surgery for arthritis.

Later examination in the Necropsy Department of the Coroner's Office revealed "2 scars in the anterior portion of the hairline and the sideburns," extending from "2 inches above the eye to the lower lobe of the ear" and "about 1 inch anterior to the ear." These were determined to be "old face-lift scars" which were "well healed."

The coroner's report, naturally, listed all substances in the room that might have contributed to his death. Despite later rumors that alcohol bottles were strewn around the room, no alcohol of any kind was noted in the report.

If any alcohol bottles were in the room, they certainly would have been reported. Instead, only two items were noted, and those were prescription bottles.

Similarly, if any suicide note was in the room it would have been noted, but no such note was found. Everything else present was noted: his wallet, watch, rings, keys, clothes, money, "misc. papers," and an airline ticket, marked "Pittsburgh-SF."

The next morning, a medical doctor at the University of California Medical Center, Seymour Farber, called and said that he was Allen's personal physician. He also said that Allen had made an appointment to meet with Farber that day because of severe knee pain. When Allen and Farber were to meet, they were to decide whether Allen should undergo another knee operation.

According to Farber, Allen had been taking "relatively large quantities of pain-killer, and medication for sleep," as the coroner's report noted. "These consisted," the report continued, "of Percodan and Seconal."

The coroner's report referred to Allen's liver as normal, except that "all of the cells contain small amounts of fat." As a result, the diagnosis was determined to be "fatty infiltration of the liver."

Presumably because alcoholism is a primary cause of such "infiltration," the cause of death was determined to be "acute alcoholism and fatty infiltration of liver." This determination seemed bolstered by the determination that a large amount of alcohol appeared to be in Allen's bloodstream.

Since that report was issued, however, we've become more aware of the wide range of potential causes of what is called fatty infiltration of the liver, causes other than alcohol. Doesn't the presence of alcohol found in his blood stream prove, however, that the cause was alcoholism?

The coroner's report, however, seems to raise more questions than provide answers. Stories have circulated that assert that the coroner later said he had lied. Even if the report is absolutely correct in its finding of blood alcohol content, the report never suggests where the alcohol could have come from, since no alcohol was found in the room.

The coroner's report says that a 0.36% blood alcohol level was found. This is an extraordinary level, high enough to cause central nervous system depression, unconsciousness, and the possibility of death. Death could have resulted from this alcohol level alone, even without the presence of medication.

Coroner Henry Turkel was cited[353] as saying that Allen's blood alcohol content was, again, 0.36 percent. According to

Turkel, this was "enough to insure a deep coma." If he really did drink this much alcohol, he must have smelled like alcohol. Alcohol should have been on his breath. Yet the coroner's report makes no mention of such conditions.

The media picked up on the coroner's report and trumpeted the news that Allen, a healing evangelist, died of not only alcoholism, but acute alcoholism. Conventional wisdom suggests that people who are hostile to the gospel tend to be glad to hear of the failings of high-profile preachers. This means, for many, that there is no room for discussion of the matter.

Even some Christians, however, jumped on the anti-Allen bandwagon once this news was disseminated. A publication called *The Gospel Guardian*, for example, said in its December 17, 1970 issue, just a few months after Allen's death, ". . . we feel pity . . . for this man's soul and the souls of the countless thousands of people misled through his teaching."[354] The publication then goes on to quote from 2 Peter 2:1-3, which contains a Biblical warning against "false prophets."

> Dear reader, take warning! Do not blindly follow any man, no matter how colorful, magnetic or persuasive he may be. . . . Always follow the divine mandate as given by the apostle John in I John 4:1 " . . . many false prophets are gone out into the world."

Even if accurate, however, the coroner's assessment leaves some significant unanswered questions. First of all, on the level of logical reasoning, fatty infiltration of the liver does not prove the presence of acute alcoholism. Secondly, presence of alcohol on one occasion does not prove alcoholism.

Further, even if the coroner's assessment was accurate, this raises some questions. If Allen drank enough alcohol to enter into a 0.36% blood alcohol level, then where was the alcohol? The coroner's report carefully noted prescription substances found in the room. Consequently, if alcohol bottles were found in the room, they surely would have been noted as well, but they were not.

Conceivably, he could have walked or taken a taxi somewhere and ingested a large amount of alcohol. If he drank enough to potentially enter into a coma or even death, however, then how did he successfully make his way back to his room?

Would a bar have allowed him to enter into this condition and, if so, how would he have navigated himself back to the hotel and into his room, where he had enough presence of mind to lock the door and to turn on the TV? His room was 418, which presumably was on the 4th floor. If he was that drunk, how did he find his way back to his room without at least hotel staff noticing his condition?

Could he have bought alcohol, brought it back to his room, consumed it, and then removed the bottles to some other location? If he had consumed that much alcohol, would he have thought to do that, let alone have possessed the ability to carry it out?

If somehow he managed to go off somewhere and essentially drink himself into oblivion and then make his way back to his room on the 4th floor, and without anyone noticing anything unusual, would such behavior have demonstrated a lifelong addiction to alcohol, or perhaps a desperate effort to deal with his knee pain?

In addition, he was taking prescription medicine that, according to descriptions of side effects, sound as though they could possibly have caused anxiety and impaired his judgement. Could that have been a factor?

If he did leave the hotel and drink, it evidently had to have been outside of his room between the time that he checked in (around 1 pm), and the time that Schwartz phoned (around 9:15 pm).

That is a substantial amount of time, and a lot could have happened in that much time, but this still does not explain how he could have either removed all the evidence (if he drank in the hotel) or how he got back to his room (if he drank outside of the hotel).

This does not prove that no alcohol was involved, but it certainly introduces unanswered questions. We are left then, with seemingly just two possible scenarios:

One scenario is that of an outrageously inebriated man getting up out of his chair in his hotel room, after having drank himself into a near coma, and carefully getting rid of all the evidence that he had been drinking.

The other scenario is that of an equally inebriated man walking or navigating cabs from a bar or liquor store back to his hotel, entering the hotel so drunk that he should have had difficulty walking without anyone doing anything about his condition. Then he had to have navigated stairs or an elevator, found his own room, unlocked the door, walked in, and turned on the TV before dying. Does either scenario sound likely?

Since neither Percodan nor Seconal were found in his room, although his doctor said they had been prescribed, could it be that Allen attempted to survive without these medications, found that the pain was too severe, left the hotel, and drank some alcohol in an effort to relieve the pain?

If so, could the interaction between alcohol and the medications he was taking have caused severe consequences? These are medications which appear to have had potential for impairing his rationality and judgment. According to medical sources, depression and confusion could have resulted from the Noludar which was found in the room.

Although Percodan and Seconal were not found in the room, Noludar was. As already noted, Allen's doctor said had he had been taking "relatively large quantities" of Percodan and Seconal.

Even if alcohol was involved, was there really any evidence that Allen had habitually drank, or that he had a history of drinking? The coroner's report suggested that some fatty deposits were found in the liver, but that the liver, for the most part, appeared normal:

> The LIVER is of normal size and shape. Its anterior edge is slightly blunted. Cut section shows the normal lobular architecture. It is a deep reddish-brown.

Another page in the coroner's department, headed "Pathology Department," contains a report from an examination of "specimens" taken from Allen's body:

GROSS DESCRIPTION

LIVER: The piece of liver has a normal capsule. The cut surface shows a tan parenchyma with normal lobular differentiation and consistency.

MICROSCOPIC DESCRIPTION

LIVER: The capsule is normal. The lobular differentiation is normal. The hepatic cells are of medium size and all of the cells contain small amounts of fat. The central veins, sinusoids and portal areas show no noteworthy findings.

DIAGNOSIS: FATTY INFILTRATION OF LIVER

CAUSE OF DEATH: ACUTE ALCOHOLISM AND FATTY INFILTRATION OF LIVER

Could the presence of some fatty deposits plus the presence of some alcohol in the blood stream have led to an unwarranted conclusion that Allen was characterized by fatty infiltration of the liver, when perhaps his medicine was to blame?

Further, since alcoholism is the most common cause of fatty infiltration of the liver, could the coroner have concluded that this was the cause when perhaps medications were to blame? Three of the four medicines he was taking, according to medical sources, all had the potential to affect the liver.

The amount of fat in liver cells was said to be "small." Although alcoholism is the most common cause of this accumulation of fat, it is not the only cause. When alcohol is not the cause, this liver condition is termed "non-alcoholic fatty liver disease," or NAFLD. This, it is said, can be caused by some medications. Even heavy soft drink consumption can cause NAFLD.

According to the American College of Gastroenterology, non-alcoholic fatty liver disease, or NAFLD, is "a very common disorder" and can involve accumulated excess fat in the liver, even if the person involved drinks "little or no alcohol." According to the same source, in a small percentage of those suffering from NAFLD, cirrhosis of the liver can even result.[355] Did Coroner Henry Turkel know this?

Martha Martin, who had attended Miracle Valley Bible College, said that she had heard that Allen did not want to take medicine for his knees, but the pain was so severe that he eventually yielded to the urgings of his sister, who strongly suggested that he take pain killers.

Referring to Urbane Leiendecker, who donated the land which became Miracle Valley, Martin said that "this is what Bro. Leiendecker told us - He wanted healing from the Lord, but his sister was pushing him to take that medication."[356] Further, regarding the medications, she said[357] that

> according to Bro. Leiendecker, Bro. Allen did not want to take those. He was a "Faith Healer" and in those days, we meant it when we BELIEVED for our healings.

She elaborated:[358]

> Bro. Allen's sister was pushing to take medicine. That was for the knee pain. Bro. Leiendecker talked to us about that. He said Bro. Allen really wanted to trust the Lord for healing, but his sister was pushing him to go to a doctor and to take medication. Bro. Leiendecker said that when Bro. Allen was on that medication, it made him whoozy and he would stagger down the halls, that's why he didn't want to take it. Bro. Leiendecker . . . said it made him seem to be drunk.

Certainly Allen was taking prescription medication that could have made it seem as though he was drunk. David Hollis referred to a story he was told in which staff members had to assist Allen, on at least one occasion, as he was in what appeared to be a drunken condition.[359]

This was long after Hollis had left Miracle Valley, however. Could it have been the result of taking three of the four medications he was taking for knee pain and resultant sleeplessness?

Again, however, the coroner claimed to have found alcohol in Allen's body. What was this based on? Is there any possibility that this could have been a matter of a false reading based on the pain killers in his system?

An individual posting to an online health forum in 2011 noted that her last three urine tests had "come back positive for ethanol alcohol," yet she said, "I do not drink at all." She mentioned several factors she thought might be factors, including taking pain medications. "I take Oxycontin and percocet for breakthrough pain," she said.[360]

Percocet is a trade name for oxycodone/paracetamol. Percodan is a trade name for aspirin and oxycodone. Percodan is one of the pain medications A.A. Allen had been taking. Even as recently as 2010, a study showed that 88% of doctors were unaware of the need for special drug abuse testing for those using oxycodone.[361] Was Turkel aware of any issues that Allen's pain killers could have had on Turkel's lab results?

The coroner's report listed two prescription medicines in Allen's room: Valium and Noludar. The day after he died, his doctor said that he was also taking Percodan and Seconal. Noludar, Percodan, and Valium each are said to have had the potential for negatively affecting the liver. If liver impairment was present, taking a barbiturate like Seconal could have been dangerous.[362]

Valium is a brand name of diazepam. According to Medline Plus, which is an online service of the U.S. National Library of Medicine at the National Institutes of Health, the possibility exists for diazepam to cause such symptoms as seizures, difficulty breathing, or irregular heartbeat.[363]

Noludar, or Methyprylon, is a sedative that has been available since the mid-1950s.[364] This drug was used in Allen's day for treating insomnia. Side effects can include the exhibiting of behavior that could be interpreted as drunkenness: confusion, dizziness, double vision, clumsiness, as well as unusual weakness, nausea, vomiting, and depression.[365]

An article in the medical journal *Digestive Diseases and Sciences*[366] reported on a case that appeared to involve liver injury as a result of taking Methyprylon (Noludar). Noludar is said to frequently cause hypertension, nausea, confusion, and nightmares, and less frequently can cause a hangover effect, "paradoxical excitation," anxiety, depression, blurred vision, acute brain syndrome, and hallucinations."[367]

Noludar should not be taken with alcohol. A 1979 report by the Institute of Medicine, Division of Mental Health and Behavioral Medicine,[368] had this to say about the interaction of Noludar with alcohol:

All of these hypnotics [Noludar and several other drugs] exhibit increased toxic effects when combined with alcohol, and many deaths, either accidental or suicidal, are attributed to the mixture.

If this was the case, and if a small amount of alcohol was found in Allen's bloodstream, why was this not noted in the coroner's report as a likely cause of death? The same report also noted[369] that when Noludar was introduced in 1954, "it was hoped to replace barbiturates and have less toxicity and lower addiction potential. Both assumptions," however, "proved to be incorrect." Further,[370]

In overdose, methyprylon may produce severe respiratory depression and coma. Although very toxic and often fatal in overdose, it does not have the unusually high mortality associated with glutehimide overdose. Patients have died from doses as low as 15 times the usual hypnotic dose, and survived amounts as high as 67 times the usual dose.

Seconal also reportedly has the potential to adversely affect the liver. If Seconal is prescribed, it is recommended that liver tests be performed to check for side effects. Seconal is a barbiturate, and overuse (as barbiturate intoxication) is sometimes confused with alcoholism.[371]

According to Medline Plus, which, again, is an online service operated by the U.S. National Library of Medicine of the National Institutes of Health, Seconal is a brand name for Secobarbital. This is a barbiturate that can be used on what Medline calls a "short-term basis"[372] for the treatment of insomnia, defined as either difficulty falling asleep or staying asleep. Perhaps Allen was having difficulty staying asleep because of the knee pain.

Valium and Noludar were found in Allen's room, but not Percodan and Seconal, yet Allen's doctor said he had been taking these drugs. This indicates a strong possibility of a major problem, a problem that certainly would have nothing to do with alcohol.

According to Medline,[373] secobarbital, such as Seconal, should ordinarily be taken only for a short period of time. Taking it for longer than two weeks can cause the drug to lose its effectiveness, and addiction can result.

More troubling, however, is Medline's statement that major issues can result if the patient stops taking secobarbital on his own. Since none of this drug was found in Allen's room when he died, it would appear extremely likely that he had stopped taking this medication without his doctor's knowledge. Medline advises,

> Do not stop taking secobarbital without talking to your doctor. Your doctor will probably decrease your dose gradually. If you suddenly stop taking secobarbital, you may develop anxiety, muscle twitching, uncontrollable shaking of your hands or fingers, weakness, dizziness, changes in vision, nausea, vomiting, . . . or you may experience more severe withdrawal symptoms such as seizures or extreme confusion.

This was not the only drug that Allen appears to have perhaps stopped taking on his own. Again, only Valium and Noludar were found in Allen's room, yet his doctor said, as noted in the coroner's report, that Allen was also taking Percodan and Seconal.

If there was any alcohol involved in some way or another, and if some was found in his bloodstream, this could have been an issue. Medline states that "Alcohol can make the side effects of secobarbital worse."

According to information Martha Martin heard from Urbane Leiendecker, Allen was reluctant to take any of these medicines. Did he stop taking Seconal on his own, and did he do so too quickly? From information supplied by Allen's doctor the morning after his death, it sounds as though his doctor expected Allen to be taking these drugs, yet Percodan and Seconal were not found in his room.

Seconal is said to be habit-forming. To suddenly stop taking Seconal after prolonged use if the person has become dependent on the drug can cause, according to one source, "delirium, convulsions, and possibly death."[374] In addition, if alcohol was taken with Seconal, severe respiratory depression or even death would be possible.[375]

Possible side effects can include "hallucinations . . . , severe depression, confusion, slow heartbeat, unusual thoughts or behavior."[376]

Similarly, a possible side effect of Noludar (Methyprylon) is said to be "paradoxical excitement."[377] In this condition, the individual experiences the opposite of the intended effect: anxiety rather than relaxation.

Percodan is the other drug that Allen's doctor said he was taking, but which was not found in his room. This, again, suggests a strong possibility that Allen was resisting taking drugs that his doctor assumed he was taking. Percodan is a prescription painkiller which may cause drowsiness and confusion. The patient taking this drug may appear to be in a daze.[378]

Percodan contains hydrocodone and oxycodone. As is the case with Seconal, Medline cautions against patients stopping their use of hydrocodone without first consulting a doctor. The reason is "you may experience withdrawal symptoms."[379] Again, as is the case with Seconal, "Your doctor will probably decrease your dose gradually," and, again, "Alcohol can make the side effects of hydrocodone worse."

In the case of oxycodone, the other ingredient in Percodan, Medline's page on this drug includes the following warning regarding oxycodone:[380]

> If you have been taking oxycodone for more than a few days, do not stop taking oxycodone suddenly. If you stop taking this medication suddenly, you may experience withdrawal symptoms such as restlessness, watery eyes,

runny nose, sneezing, yawning, sweating, chills, muscle or joint aches or pains, weakness, irritability, anxiety, depression, . . . cramps, nausea, vomiting, diarrhea, . . . fast heartbeat, and fast breathing.

Again, the advice given is that "Your doctor will probably decrease your dose gradually." The evidence in the coroner's report would seem to suggest a high likelihood that A.A. Allen may have suddenly stopped taking both Seconal (secobarbital) and Percodan (with its component drugs hydrocodone and oxycodone).

Wikipedia, in its article on secobarbitals including Seconal,[381] includes a list of 15 "famous deaths" related to use, although at least some of these apparently involved either intentional overdose or its use with alcohol. That source cites "acute Seconal intolerance" as having been responsible for the death of playwright Tennessee Williams.

Perhaps most interesting in the list, for our purposes, is the death of another evangelist, Aimee Semple McPherson. McPherson was one of the most significant and one of the best known evangelists of the 1920s and 1930s. The Foursquare denomination and the huge Angelus Temple, still in operation in Los Angeles, sprang from her efforts.

Her death in 1944 has been attributed to what has been described as an accidental overdose of Seconal, which she was taking as sleeping pills. One author claims that "Nobody knew how McPherson had acquired them."[382] In the case of McPherson, her death was viewed in the coroner's report as an accidental overdose.[383] The same author suggests that,

Because of the drug's hypnotic effect, it was possible that a person could take Seconal, forget that she had taken it, and then take more, and that may be what happened to the evangelist.

Similarly, another biographer of Aimee Semple McPherson[384] posits that:

One of the first effects of the sedative was forgetfulness, Dr. Mary Ruth Oldt testified before the coroner's jury: Sister [referring to McPherson] most likely forgot how many pills she had taken. The jury returned a verdict of accidental death - 'death was caused by shock and respiratory failure from an accidental overdose of barbital compound and a kidney ailment.'

In more recent times, a medical report noted an "alarming" increase in deaths associated with prescription drug overdoses. The first of three drugs mentioned as especially problematic was oxycodone.[385] This is one of the two essential components of Percodan, which Allen was taking in large amounts.

Included in the coroner's report was a "History of Case."This title was followed in parentheses by the heading "Supposed facts to be verified."

The deceased, aged 59 years, President of the Miracle Valley Bible College, Miracle Valley, Arizona, registered at the Jack Tarr Hotel, at 1101 Van Ness Avenue, at 12:56 PM, 6-11-70, and was assigned to room #418. According to information received from Bernard Schwartz, a friend of the deceased, and B. Morris, assistant manager of the hotel, Mr. Schwartz talked to the deceased by telephone at about 9:15 PM, 6-11-70, and, becoming alarmed, responded to the hotel, and contacted Mr. Morris. They went to the deceased's suite, and receiving no answer to knocking, entered with a passkey, and found the deceased, sitting in front of the television, apparently dead. Police and emergency service were called. Steward Machaud responded, and reported the case to this office at 11:23 PM, 6-11-70. Examination at the scene revealed the deceased to be lying on the bed, in a supine position, where emergency service had placed him, dressed in underwear only. The room temperature was warm; the thorax was warm to the touch; rigor and liver were not noticeable. There were old surgical scars on the left knee. The deceased had been treated in the past, by Dr. Misrack, for arthritis of the knee. Two prescription bottles were found alongside the television - 1 contained 10 yellow tablets and 1 contained 18 pink and white capsules. No suicide notes were found.

At 9:00 AM, 6-12-70, Dr. Seymour Farber, of University of California Medical Center, telephoned to state that he is the personal physician to the deceased, and that the deceased had an appointment made for this date with Dr. Farber, because of severe pain in the knees. A decision was to be made whether to operate on the second knee, because of continuing severe pain. The deceased had been taking relatively large quantities of pain-killer, and medication for sleep. These consisted of Percodan and Seconal. RT[386]

The report the following day by the Necropsy Department of the Coroner's Office, noted the following: "DIAGNOSIS: 1. POSSIBLE INGESTION."[387] As to the two bottles of medicine, a reported dated June 24, 1970 from the Coroner's Toxicology Department made note of what must have been these two prescriptions:

2 Rx Schumate's Pharmacy. S.F.

626113 Dr. Gordon 5-16-70

labeled Valium - 5 mgm (cont'g 10 tablets)

626114 Dr. Gordon 5-16-70

labeled Noludar - 300 mgm (cont'g 19 capsules)[388]

The death certificate submitted to the State of California regarding the death of A.A. Allen was, of course, based on the coroner's report and was, in fact, signed by the coroner. The death certificate lists the cause of death, however, as simply "ingestion of alcohol."

Whereas the coroner's report concluded that "fatty infiltration of the liver" was the result of "acute alcoholism," the death certificate went further and claimed that "ingestion of alcohol" was the actual cause of death.

No reference is made on the death certificate to claims of drug/alcohol interaction. No reference is made in either the coroner's report or the death certificate to the lack of any presence of any alcohol anywhere in Allen's room at the time of his death.

The death certificate contains the following information (the order and formatting have been changed):

• Name: Asa Alonzo Allen

• White male

• Born March 27, 1911 Arkansas

• Died 11:15 p.m., June 11, 1970, age 59

• Place of death: Jack Tar Hotel, 1101 Van Ness Avenue, San Francisco, San Francisco County, California, inside city limits

• Length of stay in county and state: transient

- Name and birthplace of father: "NFI" [no further information]
- Maiden name and birthplace of mother: "NFI"
- Citizen of USA; [Social Security number included]; Divorced
- Minister; number of years in this occupation: 40
- Name of last employing company or firm: Self; kind of industry or business: Clergy
- Usual residence: 303 Deliverance Way, Miracle Valley, Cohise [sic] County, Arizona, inside city limits
- Name and mailing address of informant: Carl Hatfield [address included]
- Coroner investigation
- Physician or coroner: Henry W. Turkel, M.D., coroner, 7th & Bryant Streets, date signed June 12, 1970
- Buried June 15, 1970, Miracle Valley, Arizona [with signature of embalmer]
- Funeral director: Bryant Mortuary [with signature of local registrar]
- Immediate cause: "Acute alcoholism and fatty infiltration of the liver. Alcohol blood level: 0.36%."
- "Natural vs accident undetermined"
- Place of injury: hotel; date of injury: June 11, 1970; hour: "? PM"
- Place of injury: 1101 Van Ness Room #418, San Francisco

The Coroner's Death

A story has circulated that asserts that Henry W. Turkel, the San Francisco coroner who signed the papers pertaining to Allen's death later said that he had lied and then committed suicide. This story appears, as far as is known, to be incorrect, however, since the coroner was reported to have died of natural causes.

This story appeared in the form of a letter, however, in the "Miracle Valley Archives Department" website of a minister attempting to revive and restore Miracle Valley after Allen's death. The letter purports to be from a Miracle Valley Bible College graduate who graduated in May 1972 and who came to Miracle Valley "right after Bro. Allen had died."

The letter claims that the student was opening the mail while working as an assistant secretary for Miracle Revival Fellowship, when a $10,000 check "fell out" of an envelope. The check, the letter claimed, was written by "a religious organization" and was made out to "the coroner that examined Bro. Allen."

The unnamed author of the letter claimed to have "worked as assistant secretary to the secretary, Ada Tye, of Miracle Revival Fellowship." The writer worked in an office, the writer said, which handled ministers' license applications and renewals. As a result, the writer said, "Our mail was not opened by the mail room." Instead, their mail was "separated and sent directly to our office."[389]

The check was supposedly being sent to Miracle Valley, uncashed, with a plea for forgiveness, according to the letter. The writer claimed that the board of directors at Miracle Valley then met and decided to send someone to meet with the coroner, but that he hung himself before this could take place.

One problem with this story is that the *Oakland Tribune*[390] in Oakland, California, reported Coroner Turkel's death, which occurred February 26, 1972, as being the result of a heart attack at the University of California Medical Center in San Francisco. The paper also noted that he had "suffered two heart attacks prior to his retirement," in addition to having had a diabetes issue.

The same paper said essentially the same thing the following day,[391] while adding that Turkel's right leg had been amputated the month before, due to "vascular problems." Lest these health issues be viewed as invented and as a cover-up, it should be noted that the heart attacks and diabetes problems were referred to in an earlier newspaper article, when Turkel retired on a disability pension in 1971 at the age of 55.[392]

Lest one would argue that the cause of Turkel's death was perhaps the subject of a cover-up, and that instead of dying of natural causes, he instead committed suicide, his death certificate does not mention suicide. In addition, no coroner's inquest into Turkel's death is indicated on his death certificate, but an autopsy was performed.

According to that certificate, Henry William Turkel died of "cardiac arrest" due to "acute myocardial infarction." This was said on the certificate to have been because of "diabetes and arteriosclerotic cardiovascular disease." What the death certificates calls "other significant conditions" are listed as "cerebral infarct, lung infection."

Turkel's health issues had been a matter of public knowledge even before he died. When he retired in 1971, for example, the press noted that he "is 55 and has had two heart attacks and suffers from diabetes."[393] Another article[394] reported his age as 56, which is the age indicated on his death certificate.

After his death, news reports indicated that he "had suffered from diabetes for several years and retired last year after two heart attacks." In addition, his right leg had been amputated earlier, during the same month in which he died, as already noted "because of vascular problems."[395] His death was reported as because of "another" heart attack[396] or "heart seizure."[397]

On the other hand, Turkel's death certificate specifically states that an autopsy was performed. Although an autopsy may be requested by a family member, at least under current law, autopsies might be performed because of questions about the cause of death. If Turkel had indeed committed suicide, however, would not the means have most likely been obvious, especially if he had hung himself as the story claims?

Henry Turkel, according to his death certificate, died in the University of California Hospital in San Francisco and his body was cremated.

Chapter 8:

A Lasting Legacy

Shortly after Allen's death, Evangelist Lenard Joe Adkins (as spelled) of Big Stone Gap, Virginia ran a large display ad in a West Virginia newspaper.[398] The reason was to present his views on the untimely death of A.A. Allen.

In his ad, Adkins spoke out against those he called "vultures and hypocrites" who rejoiced in Allen's death. He referred to them as a "group of devils" who hated Allen during his lifetime, although Allen, in Adkins' words, "got more people saved and healed in one crusade than they would in five years."

Adkins said that Allen had been criticized because of "the money and property" owned by his ministry organization. His detractors, however, according to Adkins, "have million dollar churches and thousands of dollars in radio programs." The ministry organizations associated with Allen's critics, Adkins went on, were led by "paid preachers that only give the people a 30-minute sermon twice a week."

In the view of Evangelist Adkins, the reason for the intense criticism that Allen had received was jealousy. His critics, as Adkins put it, "couldn't do the miracles that this man did." As a result, he said, they were not criticizing him as much as his anointing, "even after he died."

Paul Cunningham claimed[399] that various members of the Miracle Valley leadership at the time of Allen's death wished to collectively carry on the ministry, but that Don Stewart pushed for establishment of himself as successor. Whether accurate or not, Stewart did assume leadership at Miracle Valley after Allen's death.

Violence in the Valley: The Era of Frances Thomas at Miracle Valley

The *Chicago Tribune* noted in the early 1980s that Miracle Valley, which began as a "religious sanctuary," had become a "valley of hate." The paper cited area residents who claimed that "the only miracle" was that more people were not killed in violence which swept the site in 1982.[400]

A Chicago religious group of about 300 members, referred to as "the all-Black Christ Miracle Healing Center and Church,"[401] relocated in March of 1978[402] to Miracle Valley. The organization was headed by "Mother" Frances Thomas.

This group made headline news in 1982 when local Cochise County police entered Miracle Valley to arrest two members on traffic warrants. Apparently a third was wanted for a felony offense.[403]

News accounts are a bit sketchy, but evidently, according to police, county sheriff's office deputies were met at Miracle Valley by members with baseball bats and clubs. Forty officers then appeared the next morning with "full riot gear."[404]

That morning, local sheriff's sergeant Larry Dever was sitting in a pickup truck with a deputy, David Jones, when they found themselves surrounded by a "large crowd"[405] of people. Then, according to Dever,[406]

> They blocked the road around us. They pointed weapons at me and my partner. We told them to get back. Everything was in slow motion. There was men, women, and children. They said they were going to kill us.

Urbane Leiendecker, the man who had donated his land to Allen with which to form Miracle Valley, witnessed the event from the window of a nearby house. He said that after two deputies knocked on the door of a church member's home, "six black men" walked up and told them to get away.

When the deputies stood their ground, "a bunch of ladies and men started showing up from everywhere," according to Leiendecker. He added that "They started throwing rocks and were beating on them."[407]

Everything then, according to Leiendecker, "happened fast." He saw a teenager wielding a gun, who fired at least one shot. Two officers were hit by shotgun blasts, according to Dever.[408] The shoot-out resulted in two deaths: William Thomas, Jr., 33-year-old son of group leader Frances Thomas, and Gus Tate, who was his father-in-law.[409]

Leiendecker quickly escaped the area on his bicycle. He later said, "I think bullets were flying by me."[410] Two officers were shot, one of them being placed in a Tucson hospital in what was described as serious condition.[411] Other injuries from sticks or clubs were received by five additional officers.[412]

The clash was viewed as the culmination of racial tensions between some who were referred to as "black cult members"[413] and their white neighbors. Those tensions had surfaced at some point after the group's arrival. Expectations had been high that "all-out violence" might erupt at any point.[414]

This was not the first violence at Miracle Valley involving Mother Thomas' group. A news report issued the year before the violence said that "the 300 black members" of Thomas's group had "been at odds for almost two years" with "some 200 white Pentecostal residents."

At first, the two groups seem to have gotten along, but eventually disagreements began to surface. Those differences reportedly seemed to center around "the use of doctors and medicine, wearing certain clothes, watching television and educating the young."[415]

In 1981, the church van belonging to Thomas's group was bombed, resulting in one death and several injuries. While Thomas contended that the bombing was the work of whites, investigators had a different story: They claimed that the explosive device looked similar to devices already confiscated from Thomas' group.[416]

Frances' group, the Christ Miracle Healing Center and Church, sued local authorities for $75 million, claiming that they were victims of an unprovoked attack. Frances Thomas's daughter, also named Frances Thomas, was quoted as claiming that the police "came in and just started shooting people down like dogs." She further said that one officer wielded "a machine gun," while claiming that, in her words, "none of us had a gun or stick or nothing."[417]

Ten members of the sect housed at Miracle Valley were indicted. Charges cited 34 felony counts, including attempted murder and aggravated murder. A retired white man living at Miracle Valley was quoted as saying, "Man, it was a war over there." He said, "I ran inside and got my guns." The *Chicago Tribune* noted that no attempt was made to apprehend him or any of the other white residents at Miracle Valley.[418]

Closing Words

Lexie E. Allen, former wife of A.A. Allen, died February 7, 1990. She had been born April 6, 1916. According to her Social Security death index record, her last place of residence was Pima, Arizona, about 140 miles north of Miracle Valley. She was buried in Miracle Valley Cemetery.

Paul J. Cunningham, as noted earlier, worked with A.A. Allen up to the time of Allen's death in 1970. Cunningham died in 2010. Before he died, he noted great changes in the body of Christ since the days of Allen, and expressed frustration over the near demise of the healing revival movement which had its heyday during the 1950s and 1960s.

When told of someone having recently experienced fire in his hands, he said, "That's '50s stuff," while adding that no one talks about that anymore. According to Cunningham, the beginning years of the 21st century represented an age during which, as he put it, "most people are uninformed or ignorant of the supernatural, except for the dark side of the subject."[419]

He cautioned as to the dangers of this stance. "Because the established church has denied the supernatural, as relating to

God," according to Paul J. Cunningham, a new generation has arisen which searches for dark elements of the supernatural. By contrast, however, he indicated that "Miracles still happen, when people believe and act upon the Word of God."[420]

As Cunningham witnessed events associated with the Voice of Healing days and the great healing revival of the 1950s and 1960s, he was "awed by the visible manifestation of God's power in action," as he expressed it. But then, he said, "'the healing revival' became history."[421] As a result, he said, he found himself seeking God for manifestations of the supernatural in his own life, so that he would be able to carry out his calling.

At this writing, the buildings, or at least most of them, that once comprised A.A. Allen's ministry headquarters at Miracle Valley, are still there, although in decay. But the nothing remains of the once huge camp meetings which once prevailed at Miracle Valley, except for their lasting legacy.

Bibliography

1910 U.S. Census, household of A. O. Allen, town of Sulphur Rock, White River Township, Independence County, MO.

1920 U.S. Census, household of John Bailey, Marion Township, Jasper County, MO.

1930 U.S. Census, household of John Bailey, Lincoln Township, Lawrence County, MO.

1940 U.S. Census, household of Asa Allen, New Meadows Precinct, Adams County, ID.

"A.A. Allen," Wikipedia (online at http://en.wikipedia.org/wiki/A._A._Allen, accessed Jan. 13, 2013).

A.A. Allen & C. S. Upthegrove at Miracle Valley International Revival Center (online video) in YouTube at www.youtube.com/watch?feature=player_embedded&v=UhIkpefxUz8 and in C. S. Upthegrove website at www.csupthegrove.com/Gods_General_CSUpthegrove/CS_with_AA_Allen.html, accessed July 7, 2014.

"A.A. Allen, Faith Healer, Evangelist, Dies," *Lebanon Daily News*, Lebanon, PA, June 13, 1970, p. 2.

"A.A. Allen in Record Breaking Southern California Revival," *The Voice of Healing*, Sept. 1954, pp. 28, 29.

A.A. Allen Revivals, Inc., Appellant, v. Ellis Campbell, Jr., District Director of Internal Revenue, Appellee, 353 F.2d 89, 1965 U.S. App. Lexis 3846, United States Court of Appeals for the Fifth Circuit, November 26, 1965.

A.A. Allen Revivals, Inc. Display ad (full-page), *The Arizona Republic*, Phoenix, AZ, July 18, 1970, p. 67.

A.A. Allen Revivals, Inc. Display ad (full-page), *Tucson Daily Citizen*, Tucson, AZ, July 4, 1970, p. 10.

"About God's General" (regarding C. S. Upthegrove), from C. S. Upthegrove website at http://www.csupthegrove.com/Gods_General_CSUpthegrove/Home.html, accessed July 7, 2014.

"About Reverend Leroy Jenkins," from Rev. Leroy Jenkins website at www.leroyjenkins.com/about.php, n.d., accessed Apr. 14, 2012.

Adams, Frank C., "Article Erred" (letter to editor), *Arizona Republic*, Dec. 9, 1969, p. 7.

Adkins, Lenard Joe. Display ad, *Raleigh Register*, Beckley, WV, July 20, 1970, p. 3.

"Alcoholism Said Cause of Allen's Death," *The Altoona Mirror*, Altoona, PA, June 25, 1970, p. 10.

"Alcoholism Took Life of Evangelist Allen," *The Daily Report*, Ontario-Upland, CA, June 25, 1970, p. A-2.

Allen, A.A. *Bargain Counter Religion*. Miracle Valley, AZ: A.A. Allen Revivals, 1967.

Allen, A.A. *Deliver Me*. Miracle Valley, AZ: [A.A. Allen Revivals], n.d.

Allen, A.A. *Divorce: The Lying Demon*. [n.p.: A.A. Allen, n.d.]

Allen, A.A. *God's Guarantee to Bless and Prosper You Financially*. Miracle Valley, AZ:
A.A. Allen Revivals, Inc., 1968.

Allen, A.A. *Is It Religion or Racket? Faith or Fear?* Miracle Valley, AZ: A.A. Allen Revivals, 1967.

Allen, A.A. "Last Minute News from the Billion Souls Crusade," *The Voice of Healing*, March 1955, p. 2.

Allen, A.A. *Let My People Go!* Miracle Valley, AZ: A.A. Allen Revivals, n.d.

Allen, A.A. *The Man Whose Number is 666!* Dallas, TX: A.A. Allen, 1953.

Allen, A.A. *My Besetting Sin!* Hereford, AZ: A.A. Allen Publications, n.d. (probably about 1958-1960).

Allen, A.A.. *My Cross*. Reprinted in A.A. Allen and Lexie Allen, q.v.

Allen, A.A. *My Vision of the Destruction of America Atop Empire State Building*, Hereford, AZ: A.A. Allen Publications, 1954.

Allen, A.A. "Opening the Prisons with A.A. Allen in Latin America," *The Voice of Healing*, Sept. 1954, p. 11.

Allen, A.A. "Opening the Prisons with A.A. Allen: The Key that Opens the Prisons," *The Voice of Healing*, Dec. 1954, p. 20.

Allen, A.A. "Our Readers Speak...The Greatest Miracle I Ever Witnessed!" *Miracle Magazine*, Nov. 1955, p. 7.

Allen, A.A. Preministerial and Christian Workers' Bible College Corre-spondence Courses: Course No. 1: Health - Healing - Holiness, Lesson 3: Misconceptions in Regard to Healing (booklet). N.p.: n.d.

Allen, A.A. *Prisons with Stained Glass Windows.* Miracle Valley, AZ: A.A. Allen Revivals, 1963.

Allen, A.A. Radio programs, recordings from the Flower Pentecostal Heri-tage Center, Springfield, MO.

Allen, A.A. "A Special Notice by A.A. Allen," *The Voice of Healing,* July 1951, p. 13.

Allen, A.A. Television programs, a number of video recordings from Paul Allen, John Carver, Paul J. Cunningham, and a variety of other sources.

Allen, A.A. "This is My Heart! A Personal Message to My Radio Friends," *The Voice of Healing "Allen Revival Hour" Special Radio Edition,* 1953, p. 2.

Allen, A.A. *Thousands Saved, Healed, Delivered,* untitled four-page ministry brochure issued in conjunction with tent meetings in Rock Island, Illinois, n.d., probably 1950-1954.

Allen, A.A. Various audio recordings from a variety of sources including KamGlobal and Paul J. Cunningham.

Allen, A.A. Various television program recordings from various sources including Paul J. Cunningham, KamGlobal, Paul Allen, and YouTube.

Allen, A.A. "Will the Miracle of TV Bring to Pass the Greatest Miracle of Our Age?" *Miracle Magazine,* Oct. 1955, pp. 2-3.

Allen, A.A. *Witchcraft, Wizards and Witches.* Miracle Valley, AZ: A.A. Allen Revivals, 1968.

Allen, A.A., and Lexie Allen. *The Life and Ministry of A.A. Allen, as Told by A.A. & Lexie Allen* (ed. John W. Carver, Jr., "Containing the Full, Origi-nal Texts of: *My Cross* by A.A. Allen & *God's Man of Faith and Power* by Lexie Allen"). Westminster, MD: Faith Outreach International, 2010.

Allen, A.A., and Walter Wagner. *Born to Lose, Born to Win: An Autobiogra-phy.* Garden City, NY: Doubleday, 1970.

"Allen Campaign Brings Revival to Kentucky," *The Voice of Healing,* Sept. 1952, pp. 12-13.

Allen, Lexie. *God's Man of Faith and Power: The Life Story of A.A. Allen.* Mir-acle Valley, AZ: A.A. Allen Publications, 1954.

Allen, Lexie. *God's Man of Faith and Power: The Life Story of A.A. Allen.* Reprinted in A.A. Allen and Lexie Allen, q.v.

Allen, Lexie. "New Miracle Magazine Now Reporting Modern Miracles," *Miracle Magazine*, Oct. 1955, pp. 4-5.

Allen, Paul. *Miracles Under the Tent*, online video at www.xpmedia.com/channel/aallen, accessed Mar. 28, 2012 (identified as posted "3 years ago").

Allen, Paul, and Lexie E. Allen. *In the Shadow of Greatness: Growing Up "Allen."* (includes "Excerpt from 'God's Man of Faith and Power' by Lexie E. Allen" and "Lexie E. Allen's, *I Remember*"). N.p.: Self-published, n.d.

"Allen Preached Temperance, Died of Alcoholism," *The Arizona Republic*, Phoenix, AZ, June 25, 1970, p. 22.

"'Allen Revival Hour' Broadcast Schedule," *The Voice of Healing "Allen Revival Hour" Special Radio Edition*, 1953, pp. 2-3.

"'Allen Revival Hour' Schedule," *The Voice of Healing*, October 1954, p. 22.

"Allen Revivals Inc. Charged with Fraud," *Greeley Tribune*, Greeley, CO, May 3, 1972, p. 43.

"Allen Tent Goes to Havana, Cuba," *The Voice of Healing*, Apr. 1952, p. 11.

"Allen's Death," webpage in Melvin Harter's "Miracle Valley Archives Department" website at www.miraclevalleyarchives.org/gpage2.html, accessed June 1, 2012.

Alton Gospel Tabernacle. Display ad, *Alton Evening Telegraph*, Alton, IL, Feb. 4, 1950, p. 7.

"And the Eyes of the Blind Shall See: Testimonies from the Allen Campaigns in Cuba," *The Voice of Healing*, June 1954, p. 7.

Anonymous. "To Whom It May Concern" (undated letter written by individual claiming to have worked for Miracle Valley Bible College), "Miracle Valley Archives Department," website, http://www.miraclevalleyarchives.org/gpage2.html, accessed May 24, 2014.

"Arizona Town, 'City of God' Now Has Some 300 Residents," *The Daily Mail*, Hagerstown, MD, May 2, 1959, p. 4.

"Arizona's Newest Community Growing Fast Without Any of Usual, Ornate Frivolities," *Arizona Daily Sun*, Flagstaff, AZ, Jan. 28, 1959, p. 8.

"Arizona Revivalists Win Suit: Group Ruled Tax Exempt," *Tucson Daily Citizen*, Tucson, AZ, Oct. 19, 1963, p. 43.

"As One: Allen Revival Staff Takes New Step Too!" *Miracle Magazine*, April 1965, p. 3.

Ashbee, Edward. Helene Clausen, and Carl Pedersen, eds. *The Politics, Economics, and Culture of Mexican-U.S. Migration: Both Sides of the Border.* New York: Palgrave Macmillan, 2007, pp. 271-272.

Assemblies of God. *Minutes and Constitution with Bylaws, Revised: Assemblies of God, the Twenty-Third General Council, Seattle, Washington, September 9-14, 1949*, n.p.: The Assemblies of God, 1949.

Assemblies of God Secretariat, Personal Papers - A.A. Allen: A-G Related Material and Documents Concerning His Arrest in Knoxville, TN. At the Flower Pentecostal Heritage Center, Springfield, MO.

"Assembly Has Sermon on 'Retribution,'" *Register-Guard*, Eugene, OR, Dec. 5, 1949, p. 2.

"Assembly of God Church Continues Victory Revival," *News Letter Journal*, Newcastle, WY, Jan. 25, 1945, p. 1.

"Attend the 5th Annual TVH Convention, December 8-11, Chicago, Illinois," *The Voice of Healing*, December 1953, cover.

Balmer, Randall. *Encyclopedia of Evangelicalism.* Louisville, KY: Westminster John Knox Press, 2002, s.v. "Allen, A(sa) A(lonzo)," pp. 9-10.

"Black, White Pentecostals Feud in Ariz. Community," *Jet*, Vol. 61, No. 7, Oct. 29, 1981, p. 30.

Blumhofer, Edith L. *Aimee Semple McPherson: Everybody's Sister.* Grand Rapids, MI: Wm. B. Eerdmans Publishing Co., 1993.

Brammer, Bill. "Salvation Worries? Prostate Trouble?" *Texas Monthly*, Mar. 1973, pp. 57-61.

Brown, Candy Gunther. *Global Pentecostal and Charismatic Healing.* New York: Oxford University Press, 2011, p. 167 (f.n.).

Bryan, J.O. "Once Totally Blind - Sees Again" (letter), *The Voice of Healing*, Dec. 1951, p. 7.

"Budget Woes Could Mean No Trial in Case of 19 Miracle Valley Defendants," *Jet*, Vol. 65, No. 26, Mar. 5, 1984, p. 40.

Burcham, Mrs. Sanders, "When God Poured Oil on the Hands of My Son," Part 1, *Miracle Magazine*, Oct. 1955, p. 8; Part 2, *Miracle Magazine*, Nov. 1955, p. 10.

"Burial at Sea for Coroner Henry Turkel," *Oakland Tribune*, Oakland, CA, Feb. 28, 1972, p. 20.

Burton, R. Kent. "Miracle Valley Without the Miracle Worker," *Tucson Daily Citizen*, Tucson, AZ, Apr. 29, 1972, pp. 16-17.

California Birth Index, 1905-1995: Henry William Turkel (Jr.), at Family Search, www.familysearch.org, n.d., accessed Sept. 9, 2012.

California Death Index, 1940-1997: Asa A. Allen, at Family Search, www.familysearch.org, n.d., citing California Department of Health Services, Vital Statistics Section, Sacramento, CA, accessed Sept. 9, 2012.

California Death Index, 1940-1997: Henry W. Turkel, at Family Search, www.familysearch.org, n.d., citing California Department of Health Services, Vital Statistics Section, Sacramento, CA, accessed Sept. 9, 2012.

California Divorce Index, 1966-1984: Henry W. Turkel/Doris Chattin, Nov 1971, at Family Search, www.familysearch.org, n.d., accessed Sept. 9, 2012.

California Divorce Index, 1966-1984: Henry W. Turkel/Marialyn F. Alonso, Dec 1971, at Family Search, www.familysearch.org, n.d., accessed Sept. 9, 2012.

"Card of Thanks," *Las Vegas Daily Optic*, May 26, 1959, p. 4.

"Card of Thanks," *The New Mexican*, Santa Fe, NM, May 24, 1959, p. 17.

Carver, John W., Jr., comp., *The Life and Ministry of A.A. Allen As Told by A.A. & Lexie Allen* ("Containing the Full, Original Texts of: *My Cross* by A.A. Allen & *God's Man of Faith and Power* by Lexie Allen"), Westminster, MD: Faith Outreach International, 2010.

Castillo, Thomas Javier. "Gun Shot Valley (Work in Progress)," web page with video in the Vimeo website at http://vimeo.com/5881032, accessed Oct. 8, 2012.

Churchwell, Mary Jo. *Arizona: No Ordinary Journey*. Borrego Springs, CA: Ironwood Editions, 2007, Chapter 6: "Miracle Valley," pp. 85-100.

"'City of God' Grows in Miracle Valley," *Amarillo Globe-Times*, Amarillo, TX, May 4, 1959, p. 28, in "Healing and Revival" website.

"'City of God' is Growing in Arizona," *Galesburg Register-Mail*, Galesburg, IL, May 2, 1959, p. 7.

Clark, Mary Ann. "Mary Ann's Corner: Work with It, 'Til it's Yours!" *South End Review*, Chicago, IL, Oct. 3, 1974, p. 6.

"Coming Meetings," *Pentecostal Evangel*, Oct.15, 1950, p. 14 (regarding Gordon Kampfer).

Constitution and By-Laws of the General Council of the Assemblies of God, Including Minutes of the Eighteenth General Council Convened at Springfield, Missouri, September 7-12, 1939. Springfield, Missouri: Assemblies of God, 1939, p. 114 (regarding Earl Brotton).

Contact and schedule information, *The Voice of Healing*, Dec. 1950, p. 13; Apr.-May 1951, pp. 6-7; June 1951, pp. 6, 14; July 1951, pp. 16-17; Aug. 1951, p. 17; Sept. 1951, pp. 6, 20; Apr. 1953, pp. 4-5; Sept. 1953, pp. 4, 26; Oct. 1953, p. 26.

"The Conversation (1974): Did You Know?" in Internet Movie Database (online, accessed March 2, 2012), includes the statement, "The Jack Tarr Hotel . . . is today (2000) the Cathedral Hill Hotel located on Van Ness Avenue at Geary."

Coroner's Register, City and County of San Francisco, Record of Death: Name: Asa A. Allen, date of death June 11, 1970, with appended records from Coroner's Office, Necropsy Department, Case 1151, June 12, 1970; Coroner's Office, Pathology Department, Case 1151, June 12, 1970; Coroner's Office, Necropsy Department, Case 1151, n.d.; Coroner's Office, Toxicology Department, June 24, 1970.

"Creative Miracles in Allen Meetings," *The Voice of Healing*, Apr.-May 1951, p. 21.

Cunningham, Paul J. *The A.A. Allen I Knew* (web document accessed 2003, no further information).

Cunningham, Paul J. Personal conversations and interviews by phone, 2004-2009.

Cunningham, Paul J. Public records, Office of the County Treasurer, El Paso County, Colorado Springs, CO, Oct. 29 and Nov. 9, 2007.

Cunningham, Paul J. *Supernatural Witness*. Norman, OK: Trans World Evangelism, 2007.

Daniel, William R. *Shootout at Miracle Valley*. Tucson, AZ: Wheatmark, 2009.

Deceased minister's file listing, Lewis Earl Brotton, Flower Pentecostal Heritage Center.

Dedera, Don. "Good Morning!" ("Coffee Break" column), *The Arizona Republic*, Phoenix, AZ, Sept. 6, 1959, Sec. 2, p. 1.

"Dedicated to Gospel: Frivolities Forbidden in Arizona Church City," *Ogden State Examiner*, Ogden, UT, May 2, 1959, p. 3.

Demons Are Real Today! Hereford, AZ: A.A. Allen Publications, n.d.

Denney, Natalie. "District Faces Tax Rate Boost: Pupil Load Up and Income Down," *The Arizona Republic*, Phoenix, AZ, Apr. 9, 1965, p. C-1.

Denney, Natalie, "Tent Revivalist Center of New Feud," *The Arizona Republic*, Phoenix, AZ, Mar. 31, 1965, p. 19.

"Diazepam," in Medline Plus, U.S. National Library of Medicine, National Institutes of Health, atwww.nlm.nih.gov/medlineplus/druginfo/meds/a682047.html, Mar. 28, 2012, accessed April 14, 2012.

Display ad for A.A. Allen books, *The Voice of Healing*, March 1955, p. 25.

Display ads for A.A. Allen's ministry:

Amarillo Daily News, Amarillo, TX, Nov. 4, 1950, p. 4.

Arizona Republic, Phoenix, AZ, Jan. 3, 1959, p. 20.

The Baltimore Afro-American, Baltimore, Maryland, July 20, 1963, p. 6.

Burlington Daily Times-News, Burlington, NC, Apr. 11, 1959, p. 11.

Chicago Defender, July 4, 1964, p. unknown; Nov. 22, 1969, p. unknown.

Corpus Christi Times, Corpus Christi, TX, Sept. 21, 1965, p. 2.

The Covina Argus-Citizen, Covina, CA, May 26, 1950, p. 10.

The Delta Democrat-Times, Greenville, MS, May 23, 1952, p. 3.

El Paso Herald-Post, El Paso, TX, Sept. 25, 1965, p. 3.

The Fresno Bee, Fresno, CA, Mar. 10, 1956, p. 6-A.

The Independent, Long Beach, CA, May 14, 1949, p. 7; Nov. 24, 1956, p. A-6.

Los Angeles Times, Los Angeles, CA, July 31, 1954, p. 16; Nov. 5, 1955, p. A3; Oct. 20, 1956, p. 18; Oct. 17, 1959, p. 14; Nov. 12, 1960, p. 15; June 2, 1962, p. 14; Apr. 18, 1964, p. B9; Oct. 2, 1965, p. B9.

News Letter Journal, Newcastle, WY, Jan. 4, 1945, p. 6; Jan. 18, 1945, p. 8; Sept. 27, 1945, p. 8.

Oakland Tribune, Oakland, CA, Feb. 25, 1950, p. 5.

Pampa News, Pampa, TX, April 9, 1950, p. 10.

Press-Telegram, Long Beach, CA, April 21, 1956, p. A-5; Nov. 10, 1956, p. A-5; Nov. 17, 1956, p. A-4; Oct. 16, 1965, p. A-7.

San Antonio Express, San Antonio, TX, Apr. 30, 1955, p. 8.

Tucson Daily Citizen, Tucson, AZ, Feb. 11, 1961, p. 11.

Winnipeg Free-Press, Winnipeg, Manitoba, Mar. 30, 1959, p. 4.

Display ads for Tommy Anderson's ministry:

Daytona Beach Morning Journal, Dayton Beach, Florida, Oct. 1, 1966, p. 7

Oakland Tribune, Oakland, CA, Nov. 26, 1966, p. 8.

Display ads for Paul J. Cunningham's ministry:

The Ada Evening News, Ada, OK, Oct. 18, 1968, p. 5; May 2, 1969, p. 5.

Display ad for Dale Davis's ministry, *The Gastonia Gazette*, Gastonia, North Carolina, Aug. 6, 1966, p. 3.

Display ad for Goldia Haynes' ministry, *El Paso Herald-Post*, El Paso, Texas, July 29, 1968, sec. B, p. 4.

Display ad for Leroy Jenkins' ministry, *El Paso Herald-Post*, El Paso, TX, Nov. 21, 1972, Sec. A, p. 5.

Display ad for Gene Martin's ministry, *The Bakersfield Californian*, Bakersfield, CA, Feb. 8, 1975, p. 7.

Display ad for Miracle Valley Bible College graduation ceremony at Miracle Valley Church, *Tucson Daily Citizen*, Tucson, AZ, May 31, 1969, p. 4.

Display ad for Miracle Valley Choir, *The Arizona Republic*, Phoenix, AZ, May 3, 1969, p. 34.

Display ads for Clarence G. Mitchell's ministry:

Denton Record-Chronicle, Denton, TX, June 10, 1955, p. 6.

Big Spring Herald, Big Spring, TX, Nov. 6, 1956, p. 5; Nov. 7, 1956, p. 2-B; Nov. 8, 1956, p. 5-A; Nov. 9, 1956, p. 7-B.

Display ad for O. J. Phillips and his Miracle Church, *The Independent*, Long Beach, CA, Mar. 17, 1956, p. 7.

Display ad for Sara Steward's ministry, *Lebanon Daily News*, Lebanon, PA, May 16, 1964, p. 8.

Display ad for Don Stewart's ministry, *Oakland Tribune*, Oakland, CA, Mar. 20, 1971, p. 6-E.

Display ads for C. S. Upthegrove's ministry, *Los Angeles Times*, Oct. 15, 1966, p. B9; *News Tribune*, Ft. Pierce, FL, Jan. 13, 1963, p. 13.

Display ad for Clarine Westerby's ministry, *Arizona Republic*, Phoenix, AZ, Oct. 18, 1969, p. 34.

Display ad for XEMO, *The Independent Press-Telegram*, Long Beach, CA, Nov. 14, 1970, p. 12.

"Don Stewart's Biography," in Miracle Valley Bible College website (operated by James and Janice Cann) at http://www.miraclevalley.org/java/biographies/donstewart.html, 2002 (accessed Mar. 12, 2012).

"Drink Blamed in Death of Evangelist," *Chicago Tribune*, June 25, 1970, p. unknown.

"Driver Killed as Truck Crashes in Embankment," *Big Spring Daily Herald*, Big Spring, TX, Sept. 26, 1960, p. 1.

"Drug Tests Often Trigger False Positives," WebMD, May 28, 2010, http://www.webmd.com/news/20100528/drug-tests-often-trigger-false-positives, accessed May 24, 2014.

Dupree, Sherry Sherrod. *African-American Holiness Pentecostal Movement: An Annotated Bibliography* (Religious Information Systems Vol. 4, Garland Reference Library of Social Science, Vol. 526). New York: Garland, 1996, pp. 318, 330, 396, 547.

Duxbury, Sarah. "Cathedral Hill Hotel to Close in October," *San Francisco Business Times* (online), July 20, 2009 (regarding the former Jack Tarr Hotel; refers to the hotel as a 50-year-old hotel, identifying it as the building in which Allen died).

"Evangelist Death Laid to Alcohol," *Chronicle-Telegram*, Elyria, OH, June 25, 1970, p. 24.

"Evangelist Dies as Recording Soothes Faithful," *The Daily Report*, Ontario, CA, June 13, 1970, p. 5.

"Evangelist Dies in San Francisco," *New Castle News*, New Castle, PA, June 13, 1970, p. 9

"Evangelist Dies of Alcoholism," *The Daily Review*, Hayward, CA, June 25, 1970, p. 3.

"Evangelist, Faith Healer, Dies at 59," *The Argus*, Fremont-Newark, CA, June 13, 1970, p. 2.

"Evangelist, Faith Healer, Dies in Hotel," *The Cumberland News*, Cumberland, MD, June 13, 1970, p. 2.

"Evangelist Found Dead in West Coast Hotel," *The Anderson Herald*, Anderson, IN, June 25, 1970, p. 19.

"Evangelist Packing Hall," *Winnipeg Free Press*, Winnipeg, Manitoba, Aug. 17, 1962, p. 8.

"Evangelist Seeks Site for San Leandro Revival," *The Daily Review*, Hayward, CA, Aug. 17, 1968, p. 9.

"Evangelist Team Disagrees, Shuns Divorce," *Colorado Springs Gazette Telegraph*, Colorado Springs, Colorado, Aug. 18, 1962, pp. 1-2.

"Evangelistic Team to Lead Rally at General Assembly," *Van Nuys News*, Van Nuys, CA, Feb. 24, 1959, p. 5.

"Evangelist's Activities Raise Ire of Residents; Departure Requested," *Arizona Daily Sun*, Flagstaff, AZ, Jan. 18, 1956, p. 8.

"Evangelist's Death Eyed," *Lubbock Avalanche-Journal*, Lubbock, TX, June 25, 1970, p. 12-D.

"Evangelist's Death Laid to Alcoholism," *The Bridgeport Telegram*, Bridgeport, CT, June 25, 1970, p. 71.

"Evangelist's Death Strange Coincidence," *The Lowell Sun*, Lowell, MA, June 13, 1970, p. 12.

"Evangelist's Death, Taped Denial Ironic," *Chronicle-Telegram*, Elyria, OH, June 14, 1970, p. D-12.

"Evangelist's 'Miracle Water' Reportedly Contaminated" (regarding Leroy Jenkins), Associated Press, July 29, 2003, archived at www.webcitation. org/SwdvKgYaQ, accessed April 14, 2012.

"Ex-Coroner of S.F. Dies," *The Times*, San Mateo, CA, Feb. 28, 1972, p. 16.

"Ex-S.F. Coroner Henry Turkel Dies," *Oakland Tribune*, Oakland, CA, Feb. 27, 1972, p. 32.

"Faith Healer," *Emporia Gazette*, Emporia, KS, Mar. 7, 1969, p. 4.

"Faith Healer Fails to Show Up for Knoxville DD Trial," *Kingsport News*, Kingsport, TN, Nov. 30, 1955, p. 1.

"Faith Healer is Found Dead in Hotel Room," *Albuquerque Journal*, Albuquerque, NM, June 13, 1970, p. D-8.

"Faith Healers: Getting Back Double from God," *Time*, Mar. 7, 1969, pp. 64, 67.

"Faith Pentecostal Church" (church listing), *The Register News*, Mt. Vernon, IL, June 28, 1968, p. 13; June 29, 1968, p. 6.

Fauss, M.L. "City-Wide Allen Meeting Stirs Tyler," *The Voice of Healing*, Jan. 1952, p. 3.

Fiore, Nina (Administrative Assistant, Office of the Chief Medical Examiner, City and County of San Francisco), Letter to the author, Oct. 6, 2012 (regarding the death of Henry Turkel).

First Assembly of God Church (Pampa, Texas). Display ad, *Pampa News*, Pampa, TX, Apr. 23, 1950, p. 9.

"Former Coroner Succumbs Year After Retiring," *The Argus*, Fremont/Newark, CA, Feb. 27, 1972, p. 2.

"Former Deputy Reveals that Shootings in Miracle Valley Church Raid Were Planned," *Jet*, Vol. 64, No. 20, July 25, 1983, p. 8.

Former Ministers - Allen, A.A. (Asa A.) (ministry credentials file), Secretariat - Executive Files (Assemblies of God), Flower Pentecostal Heritage Center, Springfield, MO.

"Former Pastor Here to Hold Revival Beginning Wednesday," *Corpus Christi Times*, Corpus Christi, TX, Oct. 3, 1953, p. 2.

"Forward in Radio," *Miracle Magazine*, Oct. 1955, pp. 16-17.

"Foursquare Church Announces Revival," *The Anderson Herald*, Anderson, IN, Sept. 20, 1969, p. 18.

Fowler, Gene, and Bill Crawford. *Border Radio*. Austin, TX: University of Texas Press, 2002, pp. 320-324.

"Frivolities Are Forbidden at Miracle Valley," *Morgantown Post*, Morgantown, WV, May 2, 1959, p. 11.

"Frivolities Banned in New Arizona Religious Community," *Tucson Daily Citizen*, Jan. 28, 1959, p. 22.

"Frivolities Forbidden in Arizona Church City," *Ogden State Examiner*, Ogden, UT, May 2, 1959, p. 3.

"Frivolities, Liquor, Tobacco Banned in This Community," *The Times*, San Mateo, CA, May 9, 1959, p. 11.

"Frivolities Out in Arizona City," *Daily Globe*, Ironwood, MI, May 2, 1959, p. 2.

"Frivolities Taboo in this Community," *Corpus Christi Times*, Corpus Christi, TX, May 2, 1959, p. 3.

"Gene Martin's Biography," in the Miracle Valley Bible College website at www.miraclevalley.org, accessed Oct. 8, 2012.

"General Council Fellowship," *The Pentecostal Evangel*, April 25, 1942, p. 10.

General Council of the Assemblies of God. *Directory: Assemblies of God*, Springfield, MO: Assemblies of God, 1943, 177, 237.

[General Council of the Assemblies of God.] *Official List of the Ministers and Missionaries of the General Council of the Assemblies of God, Revised to November 15, 1942*, Springfield, MO: Headquarters [of the Assemblies of God], 1942.

Gifford, Paul. *Christianity and Politics in Doe's Liberia*. New York: Press Syndicate of the University of Cambridge, 1993, p. 201.

Goodwin, Cary, Untitled open letter regarding Paul J. Cunningham, Gather My Apostles News Letter Vol. 16, at www.apostles-gathering.com, n.d., accessed September 9, 2012.

"A Guide to the Border Radio Collection," Briscoe Center for American History, The University of Texas at Austin, at http://www.lib.utexas.edu/taro/utcah/01251/cah-01251.html, accessed Nov. 9, 2014.

Hall, J. Naaman. *And the Latter Days...: A History of Oak Cliff Assembly of God, Dallas, Texas, Now, the Oaks Assembly of God*, n.p.: J. Naaman Hall, 2009, section headed "The A.A. Allen Story," pp. 192-195.

Harrell, David Edwin, Jr. *All Things Are Possible: The Healing and Charismatic Revivals in Modern America*. Bloomington, IN: Indiana University Press, 1975.

Harrison, H.M., "I Saw the Book of Acts in Action Under the A.A. Allen Tent in Durham, N. C.," *The Voice of Healing*, Aug. 1955, pp. 12-13.

"Hear the World's Greatest Evangelists: 6th Annual 'Voice of Healing' Convention," *The Voice of Healing*, October 1954, pp. 2-3.

Hedgepeth, William, "Brother A.A. Allen on the Gospel Trail: He Feels, He Heals, & He Turns You on with God," *Look*, Oct. 7, 1969, pp. 23-31.

Heilbut, Anthony. *The Gospel Sound: Good News and Bad Times*. New York: Proscenium Publishers, 2002, p. 267.

"Held in Theft," *The Sun*, Yuma, AZ, Sept. 17, 1964, p. 7.

Hendrix, Ada, "Growth on Face Disappears" (letter), *The Voice of Healing*, Jan. 1952, p. 4.

Holliday, Pat, Miracle-Deliverance Ministry: A.A. Allen Neuclear [sic] Distruction [sic] of America - Masonry [sic] Connection, pdf document at www.remnantradio.org, n.d., accessed Sept. 9, 2012.

Hollis, David. Personal interviews by phone, Sept.17 and 24, 2012.

"Hydrocodone," in Medline Plus, U.S. National Library of Medicine, National Institutes of Health, at www.nlm.nih.gov/medlineplus/druginfo/meds/a601006.html, March 28, 2012, accessed Apr. 14, 2012.

"Hydrocodone/Oxycodone Overdose," in Medline Plus, U.S. National Library of Medicine, National Institutes of Health, at www.nlm.nih.gov/medlineplus/ency/article/007285.htm, Mar. 21, 2012, accessed Apr. 14, 2012.

"Idol Gods Thrown Away as Cubans Witness Works of Christ," *The Voice of Healing*, June 1952, p. 14.

"In Tent at Avenue S: Sunday Afternoon Service Set at Revival in City," *Galveston News*, Galveston, TX, Nov. 2, 1952, p. 5.

Institute of Medicine, Division of Mental Health and Behavioral Medicine. *Sleeping Pills, Insomnia, and Medical Practice.* Washington: National Academy of Sciences, 1979.

"Jack Coe," Wikipedia (online at http://en.wikipedia.org/wiki/Jack_Coe, accessed Jan. 13, 2013).

"John Douglas's Biography," in Miracle Valley Bible College website (operated by James and Janice Cann) at http://miraclevalley.org/java/biographies/johndouglas.html, 2002 (accessed Mar. 12, 2012).

Jones, B.V. "Pastor Reports Yakima Valley Campaign," *The Voice of Healing*, Oct. 1951, p. 10.

"Jury Unimpressed by 'Miracle,'" *The Lima News*, Lima, OH, June 28, 1963, p. 1.

"Knoxville Revival Marked by Outstanding Miracles and Unprecedented Persecution," *Miracle Magazine*, Nov. 1955, pp. 8-9.

Krapohl, Robert H., and Charles H. Lippy. *The Evangelicals: A Historical, Thematic, and Biographical Guide.* Westport, CT: Greenwood Press, 1999, pp. 70-71.

Kuehlthau, Margaret. "College Campus Quiet Again as Two-Week Revival Concludes," Tucson Daily Citizen, Tucson, AZ, July 26, 1969, p. 8.

Langevin, Diane, Personal interviews by phone, 2012.

"The Letter Bag," *Humboldt Standard*, Eureka, CA, July 15, 1958, p. 8.

"'Liberation Week' Feature of A.A. Allen Revival in El Monte, Calif.," *The Voice of Healing*, October 1954, pp. 22-23.

Lindsay, Gordon, "Convention Flashes," *The Voice of Healing*, Dec. 1954, pp. 14-16, at p. 16.

Lindsay, Gordon, "Nothing is So Convincing as Seeing a Miracle" (letter), *Miracle Magazine*, Oct. 1955, p. 5.

Lindsay, Gordon, "Report on World Revival Crusade," *The Voice of Healing*, April 1955, pp. 2-3.

"Liver Ailment Fatal to Student of Faith Healer," *Tucson Daily Citizen*, Tucson, AZ, July 10, 1963, p. 31.

Loiudice, Thomas A., Ivo Buhac, S.K. Peng, and Peter Dillard. "Hepatic Dysfunction Following Methyprylon Intoxication," *Digestive Diseases and Sciences*, Vol. 23, No. 5, pp. 533-537.

"Los Angeles Stirred by 4 History Making Revivals," *The Voice of Healing*, Nov. 1954, pp. 18-19.

Lowry, Cecil J. "Great Outpouring in Oakland, Calif. Under Allen Ministry," *The Voice of Healing*, July 1951, p. 2.

"Man Beaten at Revival Meeting," *Humboldt Standard*, Eureka, CA, Mar. 12, 1956, p. 16.

Marriage Record, Independence County, Arkansas, A. O. Allen to Miss Leonia M. Clark, Feb. 6, 1892.

Marriage Record Report No. 392, State of Colorado, Division of Vital Statistics, marriage of Asa A. Allen to Lexie Scriven, Prowers County, Colorado, Sept. 16, 1936.

Martin, Martha. Personal emails, March 2, 2012, 12:12 pm CST, Mar. 4, 2012, 11:20 am CST, regarding A.A. Allen taking medication.

Martin, William. "Amens and Imams," *Texas Monthly*, Vol. 8, No. 3, Mar. 1980, pp. 140-150.

McNeil, W.K., ed. *Encyclopedia of American Gospel Music*. New York: Taylor & Francis Group, 2005, s.v. "The Andrews Gospel Singers," pp. 11-12

Methyprylon. *Mosby's Medical, Nursing, & Allied Health Dictionary*. Elsevier, Inc., 2001, via Health Reference Center Academic, accessed Mar. 29, 2012.

Miracle Magazine, various issues, including some received from Paul J. Cunningham and others housed at the Flower Pentecostal Heritage Center.

Miracle Valley Bible College of Oklahoma, USA, (Nigeria Branch) website at kibi.tripod.com, n.d., accessed Sept. 9, 2012.

"Miracle Valley Flourishing as 'City of God,'" *Big Spring Daily Herald*, Big Spring, TX, May 8, 1959, p. 10.

"Miracle Valley is Thriving," *The Salisbury Times*, Salisbury, MD, May 2, 1959, p. 2

"Miracle Valley Named in Suit," *The Sun*, Yuma, AZ, May 1, 1972, p. 4.

"Miracles of Healing Bring History's Greatest Revivals to Mission Fields," *The Voice of Healing*, June 1952, cover.

"Miracles You'll See on Your TV," *Miracle Magazine*, Oct. 1955, pp. 6-7.

"Miraculous Cancer Healings in A.A. Allen Meetings," *The Voice of Healing*, Feb. 1952, p. 9.

Mitchell, Clarence G. *The Battle for Supernatural Ministry and Worship in Our Day*, n.d. (typescript copy from the Flower Pentecostal Heritage Center, Springfield, MO).

Mitchell, Clarence G. *Starving Sheep and Overfed Shepherds*, Miracle Valley, AZ: A.A. Allen Revivals, 1963.

Mitchell, David N. "Rev. Rogers to Become Allen Revival President," *Tucson Daily Citizen*, Tucson, AZ, June 13, 1970, p. 5.

Moore, Anna Jeanne, "Convention Diary: Account of Three-Day Meeting of TVH [The Voice of Healing] December 11-13," *The Voice of Healing*, Feb. 1952, pp. 2-3 (at p. 3).

Mullenax, Gene, and Nancy Mullenax, interview by Sid Roth, *It's Supernatural!* television program, 2001.

Mullenax, Nancy, phone conversation, 2011.

Nakai, Raymond, A.A. *Allen Revival, Civic Center, Window Rock, Arizona, July 27, 1970*. Document in Cline Library Special Collections & Archives, Northern Arizona University.

Nations, Opal Louis. "The Incredible Story of Miracle Valley," *Blues & Rhythm*, No. 213, Oct. 2006, pp. 24-27.

"No Charges to be Filed in Miracle Valley Slayings," *Jet*, Vol. 67, No. 3, Sept. 24, 1984, p. 32.

Noah, H.C. "What the Divine Healing Ministry Has Meant to the Church," *The Voice of Healing*, Jan. 1952, p. 22.

"Non-Alcoholic Fatty Liver Disease (NAFLD), American College of Gastroenterology, http://patients.gi.org/topics/fatty-liver-disease-nafld/, 2014, accessed May 24, 2014.

"Now Producing Miracles Today," *Miracle Magazine*, Oct. 1955, pp. 12-13.

Oakes, Len. *Prophetic Charisma: The Psychology of Revolutionary Religious Personalities*. Syracuse, New York: Syracuse University Press, 1997, p. 13.

Oppenhouse, Henry H. "Tuberculosis Healing Undeniably Confirmed by X-Rays" (letter), *The Voice of Healing*, Sept. 1951, p. 7.

"Oxycodone," in Medline Plus, U.S. National Library of Medicine, National Institutes of Health, at www.nlm.nih.gov/medlineplus/druginfo/meds/a682132.html, Mar. 28, 2012, accessed Apr. 14, 2012.

Petermann, Eric. "Restoring Miracle Valley to its Former Glory Latest Goal of Family's Ministry," *The Herald*, Sierra Vista, AZ, Nov. 13, 2011, pp. A1, A10.

"Photographer Chased," *Corsicana Daily Sun*, Corsicana, TX, April 3, 1956, p. 12.

Pilowsky, Daniel J., and Li-Tzy Wu, "Screening for Alcohol and Drug Use Disorders Among Adults in Primary Care: A Review," Substance Abuse Rehabilitation, Vol. 3, 2012, pp. 25-34, online in U.S. National Library of Medicine, National Institutes of Health, http://www.ncbi.nlm.nih.gov/ pmc/articles/PMC3339489/, accessed May 24, 2014.

"Postal Aide Pleads Guilty," *Tucson Daily Citizen*, Tucson, AZ, Jan. 11, 1965, p. 11.

"Postman Suspended in Theft," *Tucson Daily Citizen*, Tucson, AZ, May 2, 1973, p. 4.

Powers, Charles T., "Evangelist Practices What He Calls 'The Old-Fashioned Holy Ghost Revival,'" *Greely Tribune*, Greeley, CO, Wed., Apr. 1, 1970, p. 12.s

Quitkin, Frederic M., et al. *Current Psychotherapeutic Drugs*, 2nd ed. Philadelphia: Current Medicine, Inc., 1998.

"Radio Audience Reassured as Evangelist Lies Dead," *Leader-Times*, Kittanning, PA, June 13, 1970, p. 2.

"Re: Cathedral Hill Hotel" (review), TripAdvisor (online), January 30, 2006 (review contains the comment, "By the way, this was originally the Jack Tarr Hotel [where Allen died] - blue and white checkerboard exterior - pretty ritzy in our parents' day.")

Record of Death, City and County of San Francisco, Coroner's Register, name Asa A. Allen, Case No. 1151, June 24, 1970.

"Religious Colony Growing Rapidly," *Blytheville Courier News*, Blytheville, AR, May 2, 1959, p. 3.

"Replaced Ribs and Lung Proven by X-Ray," *Miracle Magazine*, April 1959, pp. 1, 14.

"Rev. A.A. Allen, Evangelist, Dies," *New York Times*, June 14, 1970, p. 93.

"Rev. Allen Services Conducted," *Tucson Daily Citizen*, Tucson, Arizona, June 15, 1970, p. 7.

"Rev. Clarence G. Mitchell" at Find A Grave, www.findagrave.com, Sept. 17, 2009, accessed March 2, 2014.

"Rev. Paul J. Cunningham" at Find A Grave, www.findagrave.com, May 12, 2012, accessed Sept. 9, 2012.

"Revival Starts Here on Sunday," *Hobbs News-Sun*, Hobbs, New Mexico, June 17, 1966, p. 3.

"Revivalist's 'City of God' Growing Fast," *Steubenville Herald-Star*, Steubenville, OH, May 2, 1959, p. 2.

"Revivalists 'Threatened' by Old Nick," *Tucson Daily Citizen*, Tucson, Arizona, Feb. 14, 1969, p. 12.

Rice, John R. *The Charismatic Movement*. n.p.: Sword of the Lord Publishers, 1976, pp. 212-213.

Richardson, Ray Gene, and Betty Richardson, interviewed by Jack Brown. *Lawrence County & Mount Vernon, Missouri History As Told by Ray Gene and Betty Richardson to Jack Brown on February 17, 2006* (oral history interview). Mount Vernon Founders' Day April 1, 2006 blog at mvmofounders.blogspot.com/2006/02/lawrence-county-mount-vernon-missouri.html, Feb. 17, 2006 (accessed Mar. 23, 2012).

"Roundup of Arizona News," Arizona Republic, Phoenix, AZ, Mar. 31, 1965, p. 18.

"S.F. Coroner Turkel Retires," *The Daily Review*, Hayward, CA, June 24, 1971, p. 2.

"San Leandro Hosting Revival," *The Daily Review*, Hayward, California, Oct. 5, 1968, p. 8.

Schambach, R.W. *R.W. Schambach - Giant of the Faith, A.A. Allen Testimony*, YouTube video, posted Jan. 25, 2015.

"Secobarbital," in Medline Plus, U.S. National Library of Medicine, National Institutes of Health, at www.nlm.nih.gov/medlineplus/druginfo/meds/a682386.html, Mar. 28, 2012, accessed Apr. 14, 2012.

"Secobarbital," in Wikipedia, at http://en.wikipedia.org/wiki/Secobarbital, Apr. 13, 2012, accessed Apr. 14, 2012.

"Secobarbital, Oral." *RelayClinical Education*, Vol. 2011, McKesson Health Solutions LLC, 2011), via Health Reference Center Academic, accessed Mar. 29, 2012.

"Seconal (Secobarbital) Disease Interactions," in Drugs.com at www.drugs.com/disease-interactions/secobarbital,seconal.html, n.d., accessed Mar. 29, 2012.

"Seconal Sodium," in Drugs.com at www.drugs.com/pro/seconal-sodium.html, May 2007, accessed Mar. 28, 2012.

"Seconal Sodium," in Rx List: The Internet Drug Index at www.rxlist.com/seconal-sodium-drug/overdosage-contraindications.htm, Aug. 21, 2009, accessed Mar. 28, 2012.

"Second-Hand House Moving to Get Study," *Oakland Tribune*, Oakland, CA, Feb. 14, 1962, p. E-17 (section headed "Revival").

"Sect, Deputies Clash; 2 Killed," *The Chronicle-Telegram*, Elyria, Ohio, Oct. 24, 1982, p. 1.

"Services Set, Personal Items, Deaths Reported," *Burlington Daily Times-News*, Burlington, North Carolina, Aug. 24, 1966, p. 2D.

Sharp, Herman, "Salvation, Healing Accompany Allen Preaching in Mississippi," *The Voice of Healing*, Aug. 1952, p. 10.

"'Signs Following' Lead into Broader Field for A.A. Allen" (under "News and Notes"), The Voice of Healing, Aug. 1951, p. 3.

Slaughter, Charles A., "Idaho Pastors Enthusiastically Report Allen Meeting at Nampa," *The Voice of Healing*, Nov. 1951, p. 13.

Snyder, Polly. "Airport News," *Register-Guard,* Eugene, Oregon, Apr. 20, 1950, p. 2C.

"Spokesman Sees No Harm in Allen Drinking Report," *Tucson Daily Citizen*, Tucson, AZ, June 25, 1970, p. 39.

State of California Department of Public Health, Certificate of Death: Asa Alonzo Allen, date of death June 11, 1970.

State of California Department of Public Health, Certificate of Death: Henry William Turkel, date of death Feb. 26, 1972.

Sterling, K.A., "Acute Alcoholism," *The Gospel Guardian*, Vol. 22, No. 32, Dec. 17, 1970, p. 9b.

"Summer Announcement," *The Voice of Healing*, Aug. 1954, p. 3.

"Sunday Church Services," *Alton Evening Telegraph*, Alton, Illinois, Feb. 4, 1950 p. 7.

Sutton, Matthew Avery. *Aimee Semple McPherson and the Resurrection of Christian America*. Cambridge, MA: Harvard University Press, 2007.

Tarbet, David. Display ad headed "To Hell for This?" *Big Spring Herald*, Big Spring, TX, Jan. 3, 1964, p. 5.

"Tempo to Pick in Fall at State's Miracle Valley," *Tucson Daily Citizen*, June 3, 1959, p. 1.

"Testimonies from A.A. Allen Yakima, Washington Revival," *The Voice of Healing*, October 1951, p. 21.

"These Found that Christ Still Heals Today," *The Voice of Healing*, Aug. 1952, p. 10.

This is Miracle Valley (film produced by A.A. Allen's ministry organization), n.d.

Thomas, Bob. "Miracle Valley Base for Allen Revival," *The Arizona Republic*, Phoenix, AZ, Nov. 30, 1969, p. 24-A.

This is Miracle Valley, n.d. (video documentary, apparently 1960s and produced by Allen's ministry organization).

"Thousands Throng 'Special' Nights in the A.A. Allen Campaigns," *The Voice of Healing*, July 1952, p. 18.

Thrapp, Dan L. "Summer Revivals Enter Full Swing," *Los Angeles Times*, July 24, 1954, pp. 12-13.

Tombstone of Jennie Evans, as pictured in the Find A Grave website at http://www.findagrave.com/cgi-bin/fg.cgi?page=gr&GSsr=41&GScid=1087171&GRid=6341369&, accessed Jan. 25, 2016.

"Totally Paralyzed - Healed Instantly," *The Voice of Healing*, Jan. 1953, p. 15.

Transworld Evangelism website (after Paul J. Cunningham's death) at www.transworldevangelism.com, n.d., accessed Sept. 9, 2012.

"Truck Kills One Plunging Down C-City Embankment," *The Abilene Reporter-News*, Abilene, TX, Sept. 26, 1960, p. 1.

"Two Killed as Police, Black Group Clash," *Hutchinson News*, Hutchinson, KS, Oct. 24, 1982, p. 8.

"Two Sect Members Killed in Fighting," *Spartanburg Herald-Journal*, Spartanburg, SC, Oct. 24, 1982, p. A7.

"Two Sect Members Killed in Shootout with Police in Miracle Valley, Ariz.," *Jet*, Vol. 63, No. 9, Nov. 8, 1982, pp. 8-9.

United States Social Security Death Index: Henry Turkel, Feb. 1972, at Family Search, www.familysearch.org, citing U.S. Social Security Administration, Death Master File, n.d., accessed Sept. 9, 2012.

Untitled (under "Roundup of Arizona News"), *The Arizona Republic*, Phoenix, AZ, Mar. 31, 1965, p. 18.

"Urine Test Showing Positive for Alcohol and I Don't Drink," eHealth Forum, Oct. 20, 2011, http://ehealthforum.com/health/urine-test-showing-positive-for-alcohol-and-i-dont-drink-t309163.html, accessed May 24, 2014.

Vibbert, Hansel P. "Bible Deliverance Built My Church," *The Voice of Healing*, Aug. 1954, pp. 28-29.

Vibbert, Handel P. "'Book of Acts' Manifestations Seen as A.A. Allen Ministers," *The Voice of Healing*, Jan. 1953, p. 14.

The Voice of Healing, various issues.

"Weekend Speaker," *The Gastonia Gazette*, Gastonia, NC, Sept. 18, 1969, p. 6-B.

Wyche, Otelia R., "Wyche's Column," *The Progress-Index*, Petersburg, VA, Sept. 9, 1969, p. 8.

Yates, Ronald, "Miracle Valley's True Miracle," *Chicago Tribune*, Nov. 1, 1982, p. unknown.

Zubok, Vladislav M. *A Failed Empire: The Soviet Union in the Cold War from Stalin to Gorbachev*. Chapel Hill, NC: University of North Carolina Press, 2007, p. 131.

Endnotes

1 Castillo.

2 Martin, Amens and Imams, p. 140.

3 Heilbut, p. 267.

4 Powers, Evangelist Practices.

5 Coroner's Register.

6 Powers, Evangelist Practices.

7 Balmer, p. 9.

8 Marriage Record, Feb. 6, 1892.

9 Richardson.

10 Lexie Allen, 1954, p. 9.

11 Lexie Allen, 1954, p. 9.

12 Balmer, p. 9.

13 Lexie Allen, 1954, p. 14.

14 Lexie Allen, 1954, p. 29.

15 Lexie Allen, 1954, p. 15.

16 Marriage Record Report; Evangelist Team Disagrees.

17 Deceased minister's file listing.

18 Constitution and By-Laws, 1939, p. 114.

19 Hall, p. 193.

20 Former Ministers - Allen, A.A.

21 Allen, Our Readers Speak, Nov. 1955.

22 Allen, Our Readers Speak, Nov. 1955.

23 Powers, Evangelist Practices.

24 Allen, My Besetting Sin! p. 3.

25 Allen, My Besetting Sin! p. 2.

26 General Council, 1942, p. 10.

27 General Council Fellowship.

28 General Council, 1943, p. 186.

29 General Council, 1943, p. 45.

30 Display ad, News Letter Journal, January 4, 1945.

31 Assembly of God Church Continues Victory Revival.

32 Balmer, p. 9.

33 Balmer, p. 9.

34 Hall, p. 192.

35 Display ad, The Independent, Long Beach.

36 Display ad, Oakland Tribune, Feb. 25, 1950.

37 Allen, Opening the Prisons, Aug. 1954.

38 Display ad, Oakland Tribune, March 11, 1950.

39 Sunday Church Services.

40 Alton Gospel Tabernacle.

41 Creative Miracles.

42 First Assembly of God Church.

43 Display ad, Pampa News, April 9, 1950.

44 Display ad, The Covina Argus-Citizen, May 26, 1950.

45 Display ad, Amarillo Daily News, Nov. 4, 1950.

46 Creative Miracles.

47 Contact and schedule information, The Voice of Healing, Dec. 1950, p. 13.

48 Great Outpouring in Oakland, Calif. Under Allen Ministry.

49 Contact and schedule information, The Voice of Healing, Dec. 1950, p. 13.

50 Signs Following.

51 Testimonies from . . . Yakima.

52 Bryan; see also Fauss.

53 Contact and schedule information, The Voice of Healing, Apr.-May 1951, pp. 6-7; June 1951, pp. 6, 14.

54 Jack Coe, Wikipedia; A.A. Allen, Wikipedia.

55 Contact and schedule information, The Voice of Healing, Apr.-May 1951, pp. 6-7.

56 Contact and schedule information, The Voice of Healing, July 1951, p. 17.

57 Cunningham, Personal Interview.

58 Signs Following Lead into Broader Field.

59 Signs Following.

60 Snyder; Coming Meetings.

61 General Council, pp. 177, 237.

62 Assembly Has Sermon.

63 Signs Following.

64 Pastor Reports Yakima Valley Campaign.

65 Testimonies from . . . Yakima.

66 Miraculous Cancer Healings.

67 Miraculous Cancer Healings.

68 Contact and schedule information, The Voice of Healing, Aug. 1951, p. 17.

69 Slaughter.

70 Hendrix.

71 Moore, p. 3.

72 Allen, Thousands Saved, p. 4.

73 These Found.

74 In Tent.

75 In Tent.

76 Allen, The Man Whose Number.

77 Allen, The Man Whose Number, pp. 8-9.

78 Allen, The Man Whose Number, unnumbered advertising page.

79 Vibbert, Bible Deliverance.

80 Vibbert, Bible Deliverance.

81 Vibbert, Bible Deliverance.

82 Vibbert, Bible Deliverance.

[83] Totally Paralyzed.

[84] Allen Tent Goes.

[85] Miracles of Healing.

[86] Idol Gods.

[87] Idol Gods.

[88] Idol Gods.

[89] Thousands Throng.

[90] Allen Campaign Brings.

[91] Display ad, Delta Democrat-Times.

[92] Display ad, Delta Democrat-Times.

[93] Display ad, Delta Democrat-Times.

[94] These Found.

[95] Sharp.

[96] Allen Campaign Brings.

[97] Fowler, 321; Balmer, 9.

[98] "Allen Revival Hour" Broadcast Schedule.

[99] Summer Announcement.

[100] Opening the Prisons with A.A. Allen in Latin America.

[101] And the Eyes of the Blind.

[102] Display ad, San Antonio Express.

[103] Forward in Radio.

[104] Fowler, 134, 283.

[105] This is My Heart, p. 3.

[106] Lexie Allen, God's Man, p. 3; also cited in Carver, p. 62.

[107] Allen, Deliver Me, pp. 47, 50.

[108] This is My Heart, p. 2.

[109] This is My Heart, p. 2.

[110] Contact and schedule information, Voice of Healing, Dec. 1950, p. 13.

[111] Vibbert, Book of Acts.

[112] Vibbert, Book of Acts.

[113] Contact and schedule information, Voice of Healing, Sept. 1953, p. 26.

[114] Attend the 5th Annual.

[115] Hollis, Personal interview, Sept. 24, 2012.

[116] Noah.

[117] Noah.

[118] Noah.

[119] A.A. Allen Revivals, Inc. display, Tucson Daily Citizen.

[120] Thrapp, p. 12.

[121] Los Angeles Stirred, p. 18.

[122] A.A. Allen in Record Breaking.

[123] Thrapp, p. 12.

[124] Display ad, Los Angeles Times, July 31, 1954.

[125] Lindsay, Convention Flashes.

[126] Hear the World's Greatest, p. 2.

[127] Liberation Week, p. 23.

[128] Allen, Opening the Prisons: The Key.

[129] Lindsay, Report on World, Apr. 1955.

[130] Allen, Last Minute News.

[131] Allen, Last Minute News.

[132] Cunningham, Personal conversations.

[133] Display ad for Allen books, The Voice of Healing, Mar. 1955.

[134] Display ad for Allen books, The Voice of Healing, Mar. 1955.

[135] Display ad, San Antonio Express, Apr. 30, 1955.

[136] Zubok.

[137] Assemblies of God, Minutes, 1949, p. 26.

[138] Harrison, I Saw.

[139] Miracle Magazine, Oct. 1955, front cover.

[140] Allen, Will the Miracle of TV, p. 2.

[141] Allen, Will the Miracle of TV, p. 2.

[142] Lexie Allen, New Miracle Magazine, p. 4.

143 Lindsay, Nothing is So Convincing.

144 Now Producing Miracles Today.

145 Now Producing Miracles Today.

146 Miracles You'll See, Oct. 1955, p. 6.

147 Display ad, Baltimore Afro-American.

148 Display ad for Tommy Anderson's ministry, Daytona Beach Morning Journal.

149 Hedgepeth, p. 23.

150 Allen, Thousands Saved, p. 1.

151 Allen, Thousands Saved, p. 3.

152 Balmer, p. 9.

153 Faith Healer Fails.

154 Cunningham, Personal conversation, Nov. 26, 2005.

155 Cunningham, Public records; also Cunningham, Personal conversation, Nov. 26, 2005.

156 Cunningham, Personal conversation, Nov. 26, 2005.

157 Knoxville Revival Marked.

158 Knoxville Revival Marked.

159 Knoxville Revival Marked.

160 Knoxville Revival Marked.

161 Knoxville Revival Marked.

162 Balmer, p. 9.

163 Cunningham, Personal interview.

164 Rev. A.A. Allen, Evangelist, Dies.

165 Former Ministers - Allen, A.A.

166 Cunningham, Personal conversation, Nov. 26, 2005.

167 Allen, Television programs.

168 Cunningham, Personal interview.

169 When God Poured Oil, Part 2, p. 10.

170 When God Poured Oil, Part 2, p. 10.

171 Display ad, Los Angeles Times, Nov. 5, 1955.

[172] Display ad, Los Angeles Times, Nov. 5, 1955.

[173] Evangelist's Activities Raise Ire.

[174] Evangelist's Activities Raise Ire.

[175] Evangelist's Activities Raise Ire.

[176] Cunningham, Personal conversation, Nov. 26, 2005.

[177] Cunningham, Personal conversation, Nov. 26, 2005.

[178] Display ad, Los Angeles Times, Oct. 20, 1956.

[179] Display ad, Los Angeles Times, Nov. 24, 1956.

[180] Cunningham, Personal conversation, Nov. 26, 2005.

[181] Display ad, Los Angeles Times, Oct. 20, 1956.

[182] Former Ministers - Allen, A.A.

[183] Harrell, p. 202.

[184] Balmer, p. 9.

[185] Evangelist Team Disagrees.

[186] Evangelist Team Disagrees.

[187] Evangelist Team Disagrees.

[188] Display ad, Fresno Bee, Mar. 10, 1956.

[189] Display ad, Fresno Bee, Mar. 10, 1956.

[190] Display ad, Fresno Bee, Mar. 10, 1956.

[191] Man Beaten.

[192] Display ad for O. J. Phillips and His Miracle Church.

[193] Display ad, Press-Telegram, Apr. 21, 1956.

[194] Display ad, Press-Telegram, Nov. 10, 17, 1956.

[195] John Douglas's Biography.

[196] Don Stewart's Biography.

[197] Allen, Thousands Saved, p. 4.

[198] Display ad, The Independent, Nov. 24, 1956.

[199] Photographer Chased.

[200] The Letter Bag.

[201] DuPree, p. 396.

202 Schambach, R.W. Schamback - Giant of the Faith.

203 Allen, Television programs.

204 Cunningham, Personal conversations.

205 Allen, Television programs.

206 City of God; Dedicated to Gospel; Frivolities Are Forbidden; Frivolities Out; Religious Colony.

207 This is Miracle Valley.

208 This is Miracle Valley.

209 Hollis, Personal interviews, Sept. 17, 24, 2012.

210 City of God; Arizona's Newest Community; Frivolities Taboo.

211 Faith Healers, p. 64.

212 Display ad, Arizona Republic, Jan. 3, 1959.

213 Display ad, Arizona Republic, Jan. 3, 1959.

214 City of God; Arizona's Newest Community.

215 Arizona's Newest Community; Arizona Town; "City of God" is Growing.

216 Arizona's Newest Community.

217 Langevin, Diane, Personal interviews, 2012.

218 Arizona's Newest Community; Frivolities Banned.

219 City of God.

220 DuPree, p. 396.

221 Display ad, Winnipeg Free-Press, Winnipeg, Manitoba, Mar. 30, 1959, p. 4.

222 Display ad, Burlington Daily Times-News, Apr. 11, 1959, p. 11.

223 Display ads, Winnipeg Free-Press, Winnipeg, Manitoba, Mar. 30, 1959, p. 4; and Burlington Daily Times-News, Apr. 11, 1959, p. 11.

224 Card of Thanks, The New Mexican, May 24, 1959, p. 17; Card of Thanks, Las Vegas Daily Optic, May 26, 1959, p. 4.

225 Dedera, Good Morning!

226 Gerald W. King in This is Miracle Valley.

227 This is Miracle Valley.

228 Faith Healers, p. 64.

[229] Hedgepeth, pp. 28-29.

[230] Display ad, Los Angeles Times, Oct. 17, 1959.

[231] Display ad, Los Angeles Times, Nov. 12, 1960.

[232] Faith Healers, p. 64.

[233] Mullenax, Gene, and Nancy Mullenax, interview by Sid Roth, *It's Supernatural!* television program, 2001.

[234] Mullenax, Nancy, phone conversation, 2011.

[235] "Replaced Ribs and Lung Proven by X-Ray," *Miracle Magazine*, April 1959, pp. 1, 14.

[236] About Reverend Leroy Jenkins.

[237] About Reverend Leroy Jenkins.

[238] Leroy Jenkins display ad, El Paso Herald-Post, Nov. 21, 1972.

[239] Evangelist's 'Miracle Water' . . .

[240] Gene Martin's Biography; Mary Ann Clark.

[241] Allen, Born to Lose, p. 14.

[242] Allen, Born to Lose, p. 14.

[243] Display ad, Tucson Daily Citizen, Feb. 11, 1961.

[244] Powers, Evangelist Practices.

[245] Display ad, Tucson Daily Citizen, Feb. 11, 1961.

[246] Evangelist Packing Hall.

[247] Display ad, Los Angeles Times, June 2, 1962.

[248] Allen, Let My People Go! cover.

[249] Allen, Let My People Go! p. 1.

[250] Clarence G. Mitchell, Find A Grave.

[251] Display ad, Big Spring Herald, Nov. 9, 1956.

[252] Display ad, Denton Record-Chronicle.

[253] Cunningham, Paul J., Personal interviews.

[254] Allen, Opening the Prisons with A.A. Allen, Aug. 1954.

[255] Liver Ailment Fatal.

[256] Liver Ailment Fatal.

[257] Jury Unimpressed.

258 Display ad, The Baltimore Afro-American.

259 Display ad, The Baltimore Afro-American.

260 David Tarbe.

261 Cunningham document.

262 Preministerial...Course No. 1...Lesson 3.

263 Display ad, Press-Telegram, Long Beach, Oct 16, 1965.

264 Display ad, Chicago Defender, July 4, 1964.

265 Held in Theft; Hollis, David.

266 Postal Aide Pleads Guilty.

267 Roundup of Arizona News.

268 Roundup of Arizona News.

269 Denney, Tent Revivalist Center.

270 Denney, Tent Revivalist Center.

271 Denney, District Faces Tax.

272 Adams.

273 Oakes, p. 13.

274 Oakes, p. 13.

275 Display ad, Los Angeles Times, Apr. 18, 1964.

276 Display ad for Sara Steward, Lebanon Daily News, May 16, 1964.

277 Revival Starts.

278 Services Set.

279 Faith Pentecostal Church, June 28, 29, 1968.

280 Display ad, El Paso Herald-Post, July 29, 1968.

281 Cunningham, The A.A. Allen I Knew.

282 As One: Allen Revival Staff.

283 Cunningham, The A.A. Allen I Knew.

284 Display ad, Ada Evening News, May 2, 1969.

285 Foursquare Church.

286 Tombstone of Jennie Evans.

287 Display ad, Los Angeles Times, Oct. 2, 1965.

288 Display ad, Los Angeles Times, Oct. 15, 1966.

289 About God's General.

290 About God's General.

291 A.A. Allen & C. S. Upthegrove.

292 A.A. Allen & C. S. Upthegrove.

293 Display ad, Los Angeles Times, Oct. 15, 1966.

294 Display ad, News Tribune, Jan. 13, 1963.

295 Display ad, Gastonia Gazette, Aug. 6, 1966.

296 Weekend Speaker.

297 Display ad, Arizona Republic, May 3, 1969.

298 Display ad, Arizona Republic, Oct. 18, 1969.

299 Display ad, Baltimore Afro-American.

300 Display ad, Corpus Christi Times, Sept. 21, 1965.

301 Display ad, Corpus Christi Times, Sept. 21, 1965.

302 Display ad, El Paso Herald-Post, Sept. 25, 1965.

303 Display ad, El Paso Herald-Post, Sept. 25, 1965.

304 Brammer, p. 61.

305 As One: Allen Revival Staff.

306 Display ad, Los Angeles Times, Oct. 2, 1965.

307 Allen, God's Guarantee, cover.

308 Allen, God's Guarantee, p. 1.

309 Faith Healers, p. 64.

310 Hedgepeth, p. 23.

311 Faith Healers, p. 64.

312 Hedgepeth, p. 24.

313 College Campus Quiet.

314 Thomas.

315 Display ad for Miracle Valley graduation ceremony.

316 College Campus Quiet.

317 Rev. A.A. Allen, Evangelist, Dies; Drink Blamed.

318 College Campus Quiet.

319 Cunningham, Phone conversation, Nov. 26, 2005.

320 Bob Thomas.

321 College Campus Quiet.

322 College Campus Quiet.

323 Revivalists Threatened.

324 Rev. A.A. Allen, Evangelist, Dies.

325 Powers, Evangelist Practices.

326 Evangelist Seeks Site.

327 San Leandro Hosting.

328 Hedgepeth, p. 24.

329 Powers, Evangelist Practices.

330 Powers, Evangelist Practices.

331 Rev. A.A. Allen, Evangelist, Dies.

332 Wyche.

333 Display ad, Chicago Defender, Nov. 22, 1969.

334 Rev. A.A. Allen, Evangelist, Dies.

335 Hedgepeth, p. 24.

336 Faith Healers, p. 64.

337 Rev. A.A. Allen, Evangelist, Dies.

338 Rev. A.A. Allen, Evangelist, Dies.

339 Heilbut, The Gospel Sound, p. 267.

340 Alcoholism Said Cause.

341 Alcoholism Took Life.

342 Allen Preached Temperance.

343 Evangelist Dies of Alcoholism.

344 Evangelist's Death Laid.

345 Brown, p. 167, f.n.

346 Balmer, p. 9.

347 Harrel, p. 6.

[348] Harrel, p. 26.

[349] Harrel, p. 65.

[350] Cunningham, Personal conversation, Nov. 26, 2005.

[351] Cunningham, Public records.

[352] Record of death.

[353] Evangelist Death Laid to Alcohol.

[354] Sterling.

[355] Non-Alcoholic Fatty Liver Disease (NAFLD).

[356] Martin, Mar. 2, 2012, 12:12:35 pm.

[357] Martin, Mar. 4, 2012, 11:20 am.

[358] Martin, Mar. 2, 2012, 11:25 am.

[359] Hollis, Personal interview, Sept. 24, 2012.

[360] Urine Test Showing Positive.

[361] Drug Tests Often Trigger.

[362] Seconal (Secobarbital) Disease Interactions, Drugs.com.

[363] Diazepam, Medline Plus.

[364] Institute of Medicine, p. 31.

[365] Wikipedia.

[366] Loiudice.

[367] Quitkin, p. 113.

[368] Institute of Medicine, p. 5.

[369] Institute of Medicine, p. 30.

[370] Institute of Medicine, p. 31.

[371] Seconal Sodium, RxList.

[372] Secobarbital, Medline Plus.

[373] Secobarbital, Medline Plus.

[374] Seconal Sodium, Drugs.com.

[375] Seconal (Secobarbital) Disease Interactions, Drugs.com.

[376] Secobarbital, Oral.

[377] Methyprylon, Mosby's.

[378] Hydrocodone/Oxycodone Overdose, Medline Plus.

[379] Hydrocodone, Medline Plus.

[380] Oxycodone, Medline Plus.

[381] Secobarbital, Wikipedia.

[382] Sutton, 268.

[383] Sutton, 268; Blumhofer, 8.

[384] Blumhofer, 379.

[385] Pilowsky.

[386] Coroner's Register.

[387] Coroner's Register.

[388] Coroner's Register.

[389] Anonymous, To Whom It May Concern.

[390] Ex-S.F. Coroner.

[391] Burial at Sea.

[392] S.F. Coroner Turkel Retires.

[393] S.F. Coroner Turkel Retires.

[394] Ex-S.F. Coroner.

[395] Ex-Coroner of S.F.

[396] Ex-Coroner of S.F.

[397] Former Coroner Succumbs.

[398] Adkins.

[399] Cunningham, Personal interview.

[400] Yates.

[401] Two Sect Members Killed in Shootout, p. 8; Sect, Deputies Clash.

[402] Black, White Pentecostals.

[403] Two Sect Members Killed in Fighting.

[404] Two Sect Members Killed in Shootout, p. 8.

[405] Two Sect Members Killed in Fighting.

[406] Ibid.

[407] Two Sect Members Killed in Fighting; Sect, Deputies Clash.

[408] Two Sect Members Killed in Fighting.

[409] Two Sect Members Killed in Shootout, p. 8.

[410] Two Sect Members Killed in Fighting.

[411] Two Sect Members Killed in Shootout, pp. 8-9.

[412] Ibid.; Sect, Deputies Clash.

[413] Two Sect Members Killed in Shootout, p. 9.

[414] Two Sect Members Killed in Shootout, p. 9.

[415] Black, White Pentecostals.

[416] Black, White Pentecostals.

[417] Two Sect Members Killed in Shootout, p. 9.

[418] Yates.

[419] Cunningham, Supernatural Witness, foreword.

[420] Cunningham, Supernatural Witness, foreword.

[421] Cunningham, Supernatural Witness, p. 1.

About the Author

S teven Phipps, Ph.D. has taught as a faculty member of several colleges and universities, including the University of Missouri - St. Louis and Washington University in St. Louis. Academically, he is known as a media historian, with publications in the area of media history, as well as legal and regulatory aspects of the media.

He also has a passionate interest in the history of Christian revival movements, and has amassed many thousands of documents and materials pertaining to that subject. His research tends to follow a revisionist history approach, which entails using period source materials, such as first-hand accounts and newspaper reports, to construct a fresh, new view of historical events and movements. That approach often questions and challenges assumptions of previous historians.

Steven Phipps was born again as child while living in the part of Turkey which the book of Acts refers to as the Roman province of Bithynia. He later witnessed firsthand a number of the most significant Christian movements, ministries, and groups of the last several decades, including the Charismatic Renewal and Jesus Movement of the 1970s. He has personally met various Christian leaders who played vital roles in revival movements during those years.

His doctorate is in Radio-TV-Film from the University of Missouri - Columbia. He also holds a master's degree from Southern Illinois University at Edwardsville and a B.A. from the University of Missouri - St. Louis.

He has been trained at the doctoral level in historical research methodology, and has conducted historical research at various libraries and archives across the country. He has appeared on PBS as a media historian, and his publications in the area of media studies appear in various academic journals and books. He also actively pursues extensive research into Christian history, especially concerning revivalists and revival movements.

Even in the area of revival history, his research often emphasizes the role of the media in covering revivalists and revival movements. His current research emphasizes the Voice of Healing revival of the 1950s, the ministry of healing evangelist John Alexander Dowie, and the ground-breaking roles played by various little-known Pentecostal and Holiness groups during the 19th and early 20th centuries.

PRAYER OF SALVATION

God loves you—no matter who you are, no matter what your past. God loves you so much that He gave His one and only begotten Son for you. The Bible tells us that "...whoever believes in Him shall not perish but have eternal life" (John 3:16 NIV). Jesus laid down His life and rose again so that we could spend eternity with Him in heaven and experience His absolute best on earth. If you would like to receive Jesus into your life, say the following prayer out loud and mean it from your heart.

Heavenly Father, I come to You admitting that I am a sinner. Right now, I choose to turn away from sin, and I ask You to cleanse me of all unrighteousness. I believe that Your Son, Jesus, died on the cross to take away my sins. I also believe that He rose again from the dead so that I might be forgiven of my sins and made righteous through faith in Him. I call upon the name of Jesus Christ to be the Savior and Lord of my life. Jesus, I choose to follow You and ask that You fill me with the power of the Holy Spirit. I declare that right now I am a child of God. I am free from sin and full of the righteousness of God. I am saved in Jesus' name. Amen.

If you prayed this prayer to receive Jesus Christ as your Savior for the first time, please contact us on the Web at **www.harrisonhouse.com** to receive a free book.

Or you may write to us at

Harrison House • P.O. Box 35035 • Tulsa, Oklahoma 74153

The Harrison House Vision

Proclaiming the truth and the power

Of the Gospel of Jesus Christ

With excellence;

Challenging Christians to

Live victoriously,

Grow spiritually,

Know God intimately.

Fast. Easy. Convenient.

For the latest Harrison House product information and author news, look no further than your computer. All the details on our powerful, life-changing products are just a click away. New releases, e-mail subscriptions, testimonies, monthly specials — find it all in one place. Visit **harrison**house.com today!

harrisonhouse.com